# Chocolate
## cakes

## for Weddings
## and Celebrations

# Chocolate
## cakes

## for
# Weddings
## and Celebrations

John Slattery

MEREHURST

# Contents

# Introduction

Chocolate is one of the world's best-loved foods – it is the universal language of indulgence.

The chocolate story can be traced as far back as 1502 – when Christopher Columbus landed on the island of Guanaja off the coast of Honduras, he was given a gift of cocoa beans. But it was not until 17 years later that Hernan Courtes landed on the present day Mexico where he embarked on his conquest of the Aztec empire. He met the famous emperor Montezuma, whose love of cocoa is legendary – almost as well known as his harem of 365 brides. Believing in the aphrodisiac quality of cocoa, the emperor reputedly drank up to 50 cups a day of Xocoatl (a drink based on cocoa, water, maize meal, vanilla and chilli) – a far cry from the chocolate we now know and love.

I first started to work with chocolate because I enjoyed eating it. As I developed the skills and techniques required, I learned that the medium of chocolate need not be limited to the traditionally accepted truffles and small chocolates. It could be used to create far greater things, including delicious desserts, elaborate display pieces and, of course, beautiful cakes.

Chocolate can take many forms – such as succulent paste or rich sauce.

white chocolate drops

In this book I offer you a range of creative ideas that I hope you will take and expand further, bringing chocolate work into new realms of possibility. The mediums used for finishing are very flexible – you will find that with a little experimentation, most things are interchangeable. For example, chocolate paste can be replaced by sugarpaste or marzipan or, with a little adaptation of technique, by chocolate sauce or ganache.

There are cakes in this book that are primarily wedding cakes – a trend that has grown over the past few years – but many of them can be adapted to suit almost any celebration.

What better way to spoil yourself and the ones you love than with chocolate? This book will help you to create a feast for the eyes and a treat for the taste buds. The possibilities are limited only by your imagination, so first and foremost enjoy what you do. Always remember, as long as you create something that you like and that appeals to one other person, however you achieve the result, it can never be wrong. Chocolate is a wonderful medium to work with, so enjoy the challenge.

milk chocolate cigarettes

Chocolate can take many shapes – these wafer-thin ruffles of chocolate will melt in the mouth.

# Types of chocolate

Chocolate is made by roasting cocoa beans and grinding and heating the kernels to produce cocoa mass and cocoa butter. For dark chocolate, cocoa mass, cocoa butter and sugar are mixed together to form a dough. After intensive mixing, this dough is refined by rollers. The dough is then rolled and refined to produce a very fine chocolate powder. It is at this point that, by varying the balance of ingredients, different chocolate types and flavours are created, before being turned into liquid ready to form into blocks. For milk chocolate, milk solids are added and for white chocolate, extra cocoa butter, extra sugar and milk solids are added.

Making and decorating cakes using chocolate is a real craft and you need to make sure that you are working with the best type of chocolate. Belgian chocolate is the best quality and ideal for the cakes in this book. Its high cocoa butter content and absence of added fat make it a beautifully rich but easily workable medium. Use the chocolate in block or callet (drop) form. Cooking chocolate is easy to use for pouring over cakes and it does not require tempering (see pages 16–17), but there is no comparison when it comes to taste.

# Equipment

| | |
|---|---|
| **Aerograph pen** | Used for spraying food colour onto cakes. |
| **Apple corer** | Can be used to remove a 'core' of cake in order to strengthen it with chocolate. |
| **Cake dowels** | Plastic rods that can be inserted into a cake to take the weight off the next tier. |
| **Cocktail sticks (toothpicks)** | Used for marking out dowel positions on a template. |
| **Bain-marie** | Double saucepan or a pan and glass bowl combination, used for melting chocolate. |
| **Bamboo kebab sticks** | Sticks that are used for strengthening and supporting cakes and chocolate. |
| **Cake smoother** | Used for smoothing and straightening pastes after they have been applied to the cake. |
| **Cellophane sheets** | Chocolate may be spread or piped onto these sheets and easily removed once it has dried. The shiny surface of the cellophane imparts a gloss to the surface of the chocolate. |
| **Comb scraper** | A plastic scraper with zigzag teeth, used to create patterns in chocolate, creams and icing. |
| **Cotton gloves** | Worn when handling finished chocolate pieces to prevent marking with fingerprints. |
| **Craft knife** | A very sharp, small-bladed knife used for cutting and trimming thin chocolate. |
| **Dariole moulds** | Small plant-pot-shaped moulds originally used for baking madeleine cakes, but now more commonly used as chocolate moulds. |
| **Edible gold** | Two types are used in this book. The first is a gold powder that is mixed with alcohol and can be painted onto chocolate with a small brush to pick out details. The second type is an aerosol that can be sprayed directly onto a cake or decoration surfaces, or applied with a brush after spraying onto a plate. |
| **Greaseproof (wax) paper piping bags (cones)** | Bags used for piping onto cakes. |

| | |
|---|---|
| **Hot glue gun** | Used to assemble cake stands and cake boards. |
| **Marble slab** | The traditional work surface for chocolate. Used for preparing chocolate for shaping. |
| **Metal (wallpaper) scraper** | A metal-bladed scraper with a handle, an 8cm (3in) wide blade. Used while tempering chocolate and also for producing chocolate cigarette curls. |
| **Moulds** | Available in hundreds of patterns and sizes for moulding chocolate into shapes. The few that are used in this book have been chosen for their flexibility of use, so the same mould is used in several different cakes. |
| **Notched plastic scraper** | A scraper that has been cut with a sharp blade to give a custom-made profile for spreading chocolate |
| **Paintbrush** | Small, soft brushes are used for applying colour and chocolate to cakes. A stiff bristle brush is used for applying chocolate where a 'splattered' speckle effect is required. |
| **Palette knife** | Flat-bladed knife used for spreading. |
| **Pasta roller** | Chocolate pastes are passed through these rollers to give a silky smooth texture. |

| | |
|---|---|
| **Pastry brush** | Small brush of food-grade quality, used for painting liquids onto solid foodstuffs. |
| **Piping tubes (tips)** | Nozzles used for piping decoration onto cakes. |
| **Plunger rose leaf cutter** | A semi-automatic cutter that places the vein impression onto the leaf while cutting out the shape. |
| **Rolling pin** | Used for rolling marzipan and pastes and for thinning chocolate between cellophane sheets. |
| **Savoy bag** | Canvas or disposable plastic bag used for piping chocolate onto cakes. |
| **Saw knife** | A long-bladed sharp knife with a serrated edge, 25–30cm (10–12in) in length, used for cutting through a cake without ripping. |
| **Small, sharp knife** | A straight-bladed knife used for trimming and cutting pastes and marzipan. |
| **Small sponge** | Soft natural sponge used for 'dab painting' one colour of chocolate onto another. |
| **Spacer bars** | Devices that can be used for ensuring equal spacing when layering cakes. |
| **Spirit level** | Used to check that each tier of a cake is level. |
| **Sponge roller** | Used to create extremely thin and mottled chocolate coverings. |
| **Sugarpaste (rolled fondant) ribbon strip cutter** | Used in sugarcraft for cutting fancy-edged strips of paste. |
| **Thermometer** | Used to monitor the temperature of chocolate. |
| **Turntable** | A cake decorator's turntable, used for the easy rotation of cakes while layering, covering and applying decorations. |

# BASIC TECHNIQUES

Preparing cakes before you work on them is an essential part of creating and decorating chocolate cakes for celebrations. All of the cakes in this book need to be filled and coated before they are ready to be transformed into elaborate chocolate creations and the chocolate that is used needs to be melted properly and treated correctly for successful results. Make sure that you are armed with the skills you need to achieve a stable foundation for producing truly amazing celebratory cakes.

# Melting

*Cocoa butter melts at 35°C (95°F) –*
*just lower than body temperature. To melt*
*chocolate properly, however, you need to*
*achieve a temperature of 40–45°C*
*(104–113°F). Check the manufacturer's*
*instructions for the chocolate you are*
*using. When you are melting chocolate it*
*is important that you do not overheat it –*
*chocolate burns very easily. Never melt*
*chocolate over a direct heat source – for*
*best results, use a bain-marie (a double*
*saucepan or pan and bowl combination)*
*or, with great care, a microwave oven.*

**EQUIPMENT**

Bain-marie or saucepan and glass bowl

Thermometer

## Bain-marie

*1* Heat some water in a the lower pan of
the bain-marie and put the solid chocolate
into the upper pan. (The upper pan should
not touch the surface of the water.) Use a
thermometer to keep the water at around
45–47°C (113–117°F).

*2* Keep the bain-marie open, but
make sure that the water does not
come into contact with the chocolate.
Keep stirring the chocolate as it melts –
if you stir continuously, you will be able to
distribute the heat evenly and speed up the
melting process.

*Ensure that the chocolate-containing section*
*of the bain-marie does not touch the water.*

## Microwave oven

*1* Put the solid chocolate into a
microwave-proof bowl and place it in the
centre of the microwave oven. Set the
microwave oven to a low-power setting
for 30 seconds only.

*2* Remove the bowl from the oven and
stir thoroughly, using a wooden or plastic
spoon rather than a metal one. (The heat
will be concentrated in the centre of the
bowl, so you need to spread it around.)

*3* Keep returning the bowl to the oven for
30 second bursts, stirring each time, until
the chocolate has reached 45°C (113°F).

### Melting Tip

Because of its higher milk–sugar content,
white chocolate tends to burn much
quicker than dark or milk chocolate, so
you will need to take extra care during
the melting process. Use a bain-marie
rather than a microwave oven for best
results with this type of chocolate.

# *Using moulds*

Use moulds to create multiple interesting chocolate shapes. They are easy to use and can add wonderful detail to themed cakes. The temperature of your mould should be close to that of the tempered (see pages 16–17) chocolate you are using. When creating shapes in batches, always ensure that moulds that have been refrigerated are warmed before re-use.

## Solid shapes

*1* For solid chocolate shapes, simply pipe in the right amount of tempered chocolate to fill the mould completely.

*2* Tap the mould onto the work surface to release any bubbles and refrigerate for about 20 minutes. (When you turn over the mould to release the shapes, the chocolate should be opaque and will have contracted, freeing itself from the sides of the mould.)

## Hollow shapes

*1* Fill the mould to the brim with tempered chocolate and tap it onto your work surface to release any air bubbles.

*2* Invert the mould so that the chocolate drains back into the pan, leaving a thin coating of chocolate on the sides of the mould. You can vary the thickness of the chocolate by leaving it to dry and then recoating as many times as you like.

*You can add colour to moulds by brushing a contrasting-coloured chocolate into the mould and allowing it to dry before you fill it with your main chocolate. Use white chocolate tinted with powdered food colouring to create a shade that will match the wedding or celebration.*

*Pipe in the chocolate generously so that the mould shapes are brimming.*

*You can choose from a variety of containers to make hollow chocolate shapes.*

### Mould Tips

Make sure that you keep your moulds scrupulously clean. Wash them thoroughly after use, using detergent, then rinse, dry and polish them, using soft tissue or a soft cloth. Touching the interior of moulds by hand can cause blemishes and sticking. Avoid the use of sharp metal objects, such as knives, for removing chocolate remnants, as these can damage the moulds very easily. It is preferable to use wooden spatulas or scrapers instead.

# Tempering

The process of tempering chocolate gives it various desirable properties that make it easier to work with.

- Shine – a gloss or sheen on the surface.
- Hardness – the chocolate snaps cleanly when broken.
- Good shrinkage – the chocolate contracts, thus ensuring a clean release from chocolate moulds.
- Soft melting characteristics – the chocolate melts in the mouth easily and has a smooth, not grainy, texture.

In this book, tempered chocolate is used for moulding chocolate into shapes, piping chocolate details and covering cakes with a chocolate coating (see opposite).

The three elements that are essential for well-tempered chocolate are time, movement and temperature.

After melting chocolate to 45°C (113°F), you can use either of the following methods to temper your chocolate. The first method gives very well-tempered chocolate and the second is also effective, but more difficult to get right. Remember – the temperatures are critical, so use a thermometer until you are experienced enough to recognize the moment of tempering.

## Using a marble slab

### EQUIPMENT

Marble slab or other cool surface

Metal (wallpaper) scraper

Thermometer

*1* Pour two thirds of the melted chocolate onto a marble slab or other cool surface.

*Check that the temperature of the chocolate on the marble slab has reduced to 28°C (82°F).*

*2* Spread out the chocolate and work it with a scraper until it starts to thicken very slightly. Check the temperature – it should be down to 28°C (82°F).

*3* Return the tempered chocolate to the warm chocolate and mix thoroughly until a uniform temperature of around 34°C (93°F) has been achieved.

*4* If the chocolate is still too warm, remove another smaller portion onto the cool slab, work it with the scraper, then return it to the bowl and mix in again until you have achieved the temperature you require.

## Using solid chocolate

### EQUIPMENT

Wooden spoon

Shaved or solid chocolate

Thermometer

Palette knife

*1* Stir the melted chocolate and add shaved chocolate or small pieces of solid chocolate to the bowl. (The quantity of set chocolate needed is about half as much by weight as the melted chocolate in the bowl.)

2  When the desired temperature of 33–34°C (91–93°F) has been achieved, allow the chocolate to rest for a few minutes. Stir again, then the chocolate will be ready to use.

3  Check that the chocolate is tempered correctly by dipping a palette knife about 5cm (2in) in to the chocolate. Set this onto your work surface and, if the chocolate is ready for use, it will set firm with a shine within ten minutes. If it is still soft, partially set or 'blooming' – when some of the crystals in the cocoa butter rise to the surface and give it a grey appearance – repeat the tempering process, adding a little fresh chocolate.

*Once tempered, the chocolate needs to be kept at 33–34°C (91–93°F) all the time it is being used. For small batches, you could blast the bowl with a hair dryer on a low setting to help maintain the temperature of the chocolate.*

*Tempered chocolate should be maintained at 33–34°C (91–93°F) while in use.*

## Warning Signs

*When chocolate is tempered incorrectly, it will exhibit one, or all, of the following indications – look out for them.*

■ Discolouration – a grey-white sheen or speckle, caused by the cocoa butter rising to the surface.

■ Sandiness – the chocolate has a grainy structure when broken.

■ No shrinkage – the chocolate sticks to the moulds.

■ Low melting threshold – the chocolate melts very easily on contact with the hand, because the structure is unstable.

## Coating with Tempered Chocolate

Tempered chocolate contracts when it dries, therefore if you coat a cake with it, the likelihood is that when it sets, the chocolate will contract by trying to pull inward upon itself around the cake – the result being that it will crack. You can avoid this to an extent by thinning the chocolate slightly with cocoa butter or pure vegetable oil (see Summer wedding, pages 74–77). Adding oil can sometimes have a detrimental effect on the shine, but you can compensate for this by using confectioner's varnish.

*A tempered chocolate coating can be thinned with cocoa butter or oil.*

# Layering

Layering a cake is the process of slicing it into horizontal sections and sandwiching it with filling – usually ganache (see pages 142–145). If this basic process is completed correctly, the more creative and artistic steps that follow are much easier.

In this book, cake bases of different thicknesses are required. As a general rule, the final depth of a cake base (cake plus filling) should be two thirds cake to one third filling. Round, square and shaped bases are layered in the same way.

### Tips Before you Start

■ It is easier to cut a cake that is 24 hours old than a fresh one, so bake the required cakes one day in advance if possible.

■ A chilled cake is much easier to cut than a cake at room temperature, so place cakes in plastic bags (to prevent them drying out) in the refrigerator for a few hours before slicing.

■ Always remove the 'skin' (the outer top crust) from a cake. This will generally work loose naturally. If the skin is left on the cake while it is layered, it will bond with the coating cream and create instability in the layers.

■ Using a turntable makes cake manipulation much easier.

■ For help with cutting straight, evenly spaced slices through a cake, use spacer bars at the required thickness, to guide the knife blade.

■ Always use a sharp saw-type knife to cut slices through a cake. This type of knife gives a clean cut with few crumbs.

■ Ganache and filling creams are easier to spread if they are at room temperature – 15° C (60° F) – and have been beaten to a smooth consistency (by hand or with a machine). This also prevents the cream from pulling up crumbs from the cake surface.

### INGREDIENTS

Chocolate cake(s) (see pages 138–139)

Ganache (see pages 142–145) or other filling

### EQUIPMENT

Plastic bags (one per cake)

Sharp saw knife

Spacer bars (optional)

Cake board

Turntable

Palette knife

*1* Remove the cake from its plastic bag and, using a sharp saw knife, take off the skin on top of the cake.

*2* Slice layers (about 3–4) horizontally through the cake, using spacer bars if required, and place the base layer of cake onto a cake board, then onto a turntable ready for filling.

*3* Put some filling on the centre of the base cake layer and spread it out into a flat, even layer, right up to the cake edge, using a palette knife.

*4* Place the next layer of cake on top and repeat the layering of filling and cake until you reach the required depth.

*Slice the cake carefully and evenly, using a bold, confident movement of a saw knife.*

**5** Apply a thin coating of filling to the top and sides of the cake. This stops the cake drying out and acts as 'glue' for the marzipan or paste chocolate (see pages 148–149).

*Sandwich the cake layers with ganache, spreading from the centre outwards.*

*Coat the top and sides of the cake, rotating the turntable to ensure even coverage.*

# Covering

*Applying a layer of marzipan to a cake gives it stability and creates a barrier between cake and decoration. This also provides a firm, smooth surface that is easy to work with. If you do not like marzipan, however, you can use chocolate paste (see pages 148–149), or you can omit the process entirely. In this case, though, it is vitally important that the underlying coat of ganache is very smooth (see page 19).*

### INGREDIENTS

Layered cake (see page 15)

Marzipan (or chocolate paste)

Icing (confectioner's) sugar for dusting

### EQUIPMENT

Rolling pin

Cake smoother

Small, sharp knife

*1* Use a rolling pin to roll out a piece of marzipan, large enough to cover the top and sides of the cake (and its cake board edge, if specified), with a small margin for trimming. The marzipan should be quite thin, but not so thin that it loses its stability. Use a little icing (confectioner's) sugar to prevent the marzipan from sticking to the rolling pin or work surface.

*2* Drape the thin piece of marzipan carefully over the cake, (wrapping the marzipan around the rolling pin before you lift it may be helpful – then you can unroll it smoothly and gradually over the cake without stretching it).

*3* Starting at the top centre, use a cake smoother to flatten the marzipan over the cake neatly. Use a circular motion with the cake smoother and press the marzipan into position, eliminating any air that may be trapped beneath.

*4* Smooth the top of the cake, then work down the sides, ensuring a smooth, creaseless coating. Trim off any excess marzipan from around the base of the cake using a small, sharp knife. Run the smoother around the cake again to make sure that the sides are completely straight and even before you continue to work on the cake.

*Make sure that the cake is completely covered with a thin layer of marzipan.*

*Chocolate paste does the same job as a covering of marzipan.*

# Levelling

When you have covered a cake, you must ensure that the surface is perfectly level. That way you can be sure that the finished cake is ready for decoration.

## EQUIPMENT

Cellophane

Cake board

Spirit level

Weight

*1* Lay a sheet of cellophane on top of the cake and put a cake board on top of this. Put the spirit level in position and apply pressure to the board to level it, if required.

*2* Put a weight in position and leave the cake to stand overnight. Then, remove the cellophane and allow the marzipan to dry.

*Accurate levelling ensures that tiered cakes sit straight and even.*

*By using a spirit level, you can guarantee that your cake is completely flat.*

# CAKES and CENTREPIECES

*Most of the incredible cakes in this book take several days to make – from start to finish – so make sure that you leave yourself plenty of time before the day of your celebration. Once you have finished making your beautiful chocolate cake, you should store it at room temperature – 15°C (60°F) – until you are ready to present it. Only cakes containing fresh cream need to be refrigerated.*

*This type of cake is very often served as the dessert at a wedding reception. It sits well with a variety of accompaniments, including fresh summer berry fruits, a coulis, ice cream, fresh pouring cream, whipped cream with amaretto and, of course, warm chocolate sauce. Always use the best quality soft fruits.*

# Summer fruits

## CAKE AND DECORATION

4.5kg (10lb) white chocolate (to make 500 white chocolate cigarette curls)

30cm (12in), 23cm (9in), 15cm (6in) and 8cm (3in) round chocolate cakes (see pages 138–139)

30cm (12in), 23cm (9in), 15cm (6in) and 8cm (3in) round cake boards

45cm (18in) round cake board for the base

2.1kg (4lb 8oz) ganache (see pages 142–145)

2.75kg (6lb) marzipan

2.5kg (5lb 8oz) white chocolate sauce (see pages 146–147)

Gold ribbon for board edge

3 punnets each of raspberries, redcurrants and blackberries

2 punnets strawberries

Fresh ivy or mint leaves (optional)

## EQUIPMENT

Marble slab or metal surface

Metal (wallpaper) scraper

Equipment for layering, covering and levelling (see pages 18–21)

Round paper templates of 30cm (12in), 23cm (9in) and 15cm (6in)

12 cake dowels

Cocktail stick (toothpick)

*1* For best results, make the curls several hours before they are required. A quantity of 450g (1lb) of chocolate produces about 50 cigarette curls. Make the chocolate curls in batches, using approximately 450g (1lb) untempered melted chocolate at a time. Spread the chocolate thinly onto a room temperature marble slab using a metal (wallpaper) scraper. Massage the chocolate with a forward and backward movement of the scraper until it becomes firm.

*2* Using the metal scraper at a 45 degree angle, push the chocolate away from you to form a cigarette curl of the desired size (the height of your cakes).

*Massage the chocolate backwards and forwards, spreading it as it firms up.*

*Use the scraper to push the chocolate away from you, allowing it to curl.*

*3* Layer the cakes and fill and coat with ganache (see pages 18–19). Place each cake on its corresponding board, then onto another larger spare cake board, to work on. Cover the cakes with marzipan (see page 20), being sure to also cover the board edges. Level (see page 21), then leave to stand for 24 hours to firm up.

*4* Cut out paper templates of the bottom and middle cake sizes. Mark the position of the dowels on the templates by folding the circles in half, then half again. While folded, measure the centre point on both straight sides and mark firmly with a pencil so that, when unfolded, four equally spaced dots are marked. Place the template on the cake. Prick through each template to mark the dowel positions with a cocktail stick (toothpick).

*5* Remove the templates and insert the dowels into the cakes at these points. Mark the dowels where they meet the surface of the cake, then pull them out and cut them off at this mark. Re-insert the dowels, then place the cakes on top of each other. There is no need to secure these together as the chocolate coating will hold them in place perfectly.

*6* Warm the chocolate sauce to about 35°C (95°F). Stand the cake on a turntable, placing it on a baking sheet to catch the drips. Pour the sauce over the top tier in a circular motion, so that the sauce cascades evenly down over the cake.

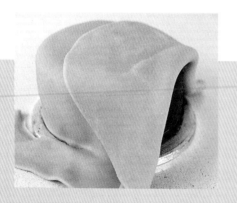

*Cover the cake with a layer of marzipan and trim off the excess.*

*Using a paper template for the bottom and middle tiers, mark the position of each dowel.*

*Insert the dowel into the cake and mark where the dowel meets the cake surface.*

*7* Gently lift and tap the whole cake to help the sauce form an even coating over both the cake and the base board – you could use a palette knife to aid this process. Leave the cake to stand for about 30 minutes, to enable the sauce to firm a little.

*8* Carefully place the chocolate curls into position around the sides of the cakes. Leave to stand overnight to firm up completely. Trim excess sauce from the board edge using the back of a knife. Apply the gold ribbon around the board edge, fixing into place with glue.

*9* Store the cake at room temperature – 15°C (60°F) – until ready to serve. Arrange the fruit on the cake just before serving and decorate with ivy or mint, if desired.

## Variations

*Several different styles of finish can be created by altering one or several of the components.*

■ Use a different colour chocolate.

■ Use four colours of chocolate curls graduated upwards.

■ Loop gold ribbons with trailing ends and intersperse with golden mini-apples and orange physallis.

■ Arrange a trail of ivy simply from tier to tier.

■ Brush the top edges of the cigarette curls with edible gold or silver, then drape gold or silver strings of beads around the cakes.

■ Fill all the edges and ledges of the cake with fresh raspberries.

milk and white chocolate cigarette curls

milk chocolate cigarette curls

*Pour the chocolate sauce over the top tier in a circular motion for even coating.*

*Place the chocolate cigarette curls neatly around the sides of each cake.*

## Chocolate Tip

As with most chocolate-finished cakes, this one can be made several days in advance and should be stored at room temperature. Keep the fruit refrigerated, and position it on the cake as near as possible to the time of serving. This will keep the fruit fresh and prevent it from 'bleeding' and staining the cake.

# Strawberry bowl centrepiece

This stunning centrepiece filled with fresh strawberries dipped in stripy white chocolate will fit beautifully with the Summer fruits cake (see pages 24–27). It will also be perfect for a summer wedding or just an afternoon party in the garden, as you can furnish each table with a bowl. The delicious combination of strawberries and different-coloured chocolate, presented beautifully in a mouth-watering edible bowl, will truly impress your guests.

The chocolate bowls can be made well in advance of the occasion, but the strawberries must be dipped on the day. Choose only firm, dry fruit that is the same colour right through, with fresh-looking greenery and stalks.

The fruit shown here is dipped into white chocolate marbled with milk chocolate, but you can use any combination or single-colour chocolate you desire. This recipe produces one centrepiece, but increase the quantities to make as many as you choose.

**1** Temper the milk chocolate (see pages 16–17) and use a half-sphere mould to make a bowl shape using 140g (5oz) of the chocolate (see page 15). You may need to use two coats of chocolate for maximum strength. Refrigerate for about 20 minutes, then remove the half-sphere shapes, handling carefully so as not to put fingerprints on them.

**2** Use some milk chocolate to pipe 4cm (1½in) discs of chocolate onto greaseproof (wax) paper. Sit the half-spheres onto these discs to create bowls with bases and hold in position until the chocolate thickens and can support the dishes. You can decorate these if you like – a small bulb of chocolate around the top rim will look great. You could even use a contrasting-coloured chocolate piped onto the side of the bowl as a border. Store at 15°C (60°F).

### INGREDIENTS

160g (5¾oz) milk chocolate

10 strawberries

150g (5¼oz) white chocolate

### EQUIPMENT

Half-sphere mould

Equipment for tempering (see pages 16–17)

Greaseproof (wax) paper piping bags (cones)

**3** Do not hull the strawberries, but wash them in cold water and dry each thoroughly. Temper the white chocolate and put in a bowl. Pour the remaining tempered milk chocolate into a greaseproof paper piping bag (cone) and pipe three lines across the white chocolate.

**4** Place a strawberry onto the end of a small fork and dip it into the bowl of chocolate, under the milk stripes. Bring up the strawberry, so that it is two-thirds covered in white chocolate, with thin milk chocolate stripes across. Keep applying the milk-chocolate piped lines across the white chocolate as often as necessary, as you continue to dip the strawberries.

Pour in the tempered chocolate to fill the half-sphere mould completely.

Pour the chocolate back into the bowl, leaving a coating of chocolate inside the mould.

After refrigeration, the bowl shape should emerge effortlessly from the mould.

*5* Place each single strawberry onto a piece of greaseproof paper until the chocolate is set completely. Arrange the strawberries into each chocolate bowl and place the finished centrepiece on the table.

*Handle the chocolate carefully as you adhere the disc base to the bowl.*

*Keep piping in the milk chocolate so that each of the strawberries has a stripy coating.*

*Once dry, arrange the succulent stripy strawberries in their chocolate bowl.*

*A three-tier cake in the American 'stacked' style, decorated with chocolate roses and a beautiful marbled chocolate drape made from dark, milk and white chocolate pastes. This spectacular cake, with its combination of chocolate textures, is ideal for any celebration.*

# Rose drape

## CAKE AND DECORATION

30cm (12in), 23cm (9in) and 15cm (6in) round chocolate cakes (see pages 138–139)

1.4kg (3lb) ganache

30cm (12in), 23cm (9in) and 15cm (6in) round cake boards

45cm (18in) round cake board for the base

2.4kg (5lb) white marzipan

55g (2oz) clear alcohol (such as gin or vodka)

2.5kg (5lb 8oz) white chocolate paste (see pages 148–149)

225g (8oz) white chocolate

340g (12oz) dark chocolate

285g (10oz) dark chocolate paste (see pages 148–149)

400g (14oz) milk chocolate paste (see pages 148–149)

Greaseproof (wax) paper piping bags (cones)

Ribbon for board edge

9 large roses (11 petals), 9 smaller roses (7 petals) and 9 assorted buds (2 or 4 petals) and 25 leaves (see pages 36–37).

## EQUIPMENT

Equipment for layering, covering and levelling (see pages 18–21)

8 dowel rods

Number 2 plain tube (tip)

Number 1 plain tube (tip)

**1** Cut each cake into three slices and layer (see pages 18–19). Place the cakes on their boards. Roll out 1.25kg (2½lb) of the marzipan – this will be sufficient to cover the 30cm (12in) cake (top, sides and cake board included) in one piece. Cover the cake with the marzipan (see page 20). Repeat for the remaining two cakes, using 680g (1½lb) and 450g (1lb) of marzipan, respectively. Level (see page 21) and allow the cakes to firm overnight.

**2** Brush the three marzipan-covered cakes with clear alcohol in order to create a sticky surface for the chocolate paste to adhere to. Roll out 1.25kg (2½lb) of white chocolate paste

*Cover all three cakes with a thin marzipan layer, making sure that the finish is smooth and flat.*

*Pipe the white chocolate so that the beads nestle into the joins between the cakes.*

and apply to the cake in the same way as for the marzipan, using a cake smoother in order to create a flat, even surface. Repeat for the remaining two cakes, using 680g (1½lb) and 450g (1lb) of chocolate paste, respectively. Allow the cakes to dry overnight.

3 Insert dowel rods into the base and middle tiers (see page 26). Stack the three cakes together, ensuring that they are centrally placed on top of each other.

4 Melt half the quantity of white chocolate and turn it into piping chocolate by adding a couple of drops of water and stirring well. Be careful not to add too much water as it would over-thicken the chocolate and render it totally useless. Place a number 2 plain tube (tip) into a greaseproof (wax) paper piping bag (cone). Fill half the bag with piping chocolate and proceed to pipe small bulbs around the base of each cake. Mix the next quantity of piping chocolate as required (it is best to mix the piping chocolate in small batches as it has quite a short working life before it becomes too stiff to pipe with).

5 Melt the dark chocolate and thicken it slightly to a piping chocolate consistency by adding a couple of drops of water. Place the melted dark chocolate into a greaseproof paper bag equipped this time with a number 1 plain tube. Pipe a delicate decorative design around the base of each tier. Feel free to use the design in the photograph shown or, better still, you can

Combine the chocolate pastes, then roll them out into a long oblong shape.

Drape the marbled paste carefully over the cake, so that it resembles fabric.

create your own. If you are making the cake for a wedding, you could even add a personal touch to your design by picking out some beautiful embroidery details from the wedding dress and reproducing them on the cake.

*6*  To create the drape, roll together 225g (8oz) each of the dark, milk and white chocolate pastes. Knead until all three pastes are slightly mingled, then cut through the roll and stand the halves closely side by side, with the cut ends uppermost. Flatten both halves with the heel of your hand. Using a little icing (confectioner's) sugar to dust with, roll out the two pieces of paste into one oblong shape that is 40cm x 15cm (16in x 6in) in length and approximately 5mm (¼in) in thickness.

*7*  Arrange the chocolate drape into position starting at the top of the cake. Fold and tuck the paste, working downwards to recreate the look of a fabric that has been softly folded in place. Secure the drape in position with a little water.

*8*  Arrange all of the flowers and the leaves carefully onto the cake, securing them into place with either a little melted chocolate sauce or some tempered chocolate. Start with the larger flowers and intersperse the smaller ones around them for the most natural look. To complete the cake, apply a matching ribbon to the base board.

*Secure the chocolate roses onto the drape, using a little sauce or tempered chocolate.*

*The rose arrangement should look random and natural, with assorted shapes and sizes.*

### Chocolate Tip

You can enhance the sheen on the chocolate roses by coating them with cocoa butter or confectioner's varnish thinned slightly with a little clear alcohol. This will really bring the flowers to life.

## CAKE AND DECORATION

30cm (12in), 23cm (9in) and 15cm (6in) round chocolate cakes (see pages 138–139)

40cm (16in) 32cm (13in) and 25cm (10in) round cake boards

2.5kg (5½lb) ganache

1.6kg (3½lb) marzipan

350g (12½oz) dark chocolate paste (see pages 148–149)

500g (1lb 2oz) milk chocolate paste (see pages 148–149)

300g (10½oz) white chocolate paste (see pages 148–149)

## EQUIPMENT

Equipment for layering, covering and levelling (see pages 18–21)

Plastic bags

2cm (¾in) rose leaf plunger cutter

*This cake is blooming with chocolate paste roses. The milk chocolate flowers with their dark chocolate leaves bring the cake to life, but are, in fact, much simpler to make than they seem. You can vary the sizes of the roses, if you like, and use different-coloured paste – to create a natural feel.*

# Roses and leaves

*1* Layer the cakes, fill and coat with 900g (2lb) of the ganache, then cover with marzipan and level (see pages 18–21). Allow the marzipan to dry overnight, then stack the cakes, warm the remaining ganache and apply to the cakes, using a palette knife to create a rough finish.

*2* Roll the chocolate pastes into 'sausages' of 1.5cm (⅝in) diameter. Cut into 5mm (¼in) slices. Lay these in a plastic bag, place one thumb behind a slice and, with the other, press out the paste on three sides. Prepare petals for 20 dark, 30 milk and 20 white roses. Roll one slice into a cone, then layer with petals (see below). Make the leaves (see below) and apply to the cake.

*Lay the slices of chocolate paste into a plastic bag and squeeze them into petal shapes.*

*Wrap the petals around one another to establish the shape of a blooming rose and dry overnight.*

*Roll out the dark chocolate paste to 3mm (⅛in) thickness. Cut out 50 leaves and allow to dry.*

*This pyramid of profiteroles is the traditional centrepiece for a French wedding reception, but can also be used as a striking dessert at any other celebration. This variation of the croquembouche uses chocolate not only in the filling for the choux balls, but also to hold the pyramid together.*

# Croquembouche

### CAKE AND DECORATION

115g (4oz) unsalted butter at 15°C (60°F), cubed

225 g (8oz or 2 cups) plain (all-purpose) flour

Pinch of salt

7 large eggs

575ml (19fl oz) full-cream milk

80g (3oz) caster (superfine) sugar, plus extra for sprinkling

30g (1oz or ¼ cup) cornflour (cornstarch)

225g (8oz) dark chocolate

1litre 150ml (38 fl oz) fresh whipping cream

800g (1lb 12oz) white chocolate

30cm (12in) cake board

Star template (see pages 152–155)

Edible gold spray or paint

3m (10ft) gold wire-edged ribbon

### EQUIPMENT

Savoy bags

2cm (¾in) and 1cm (½in) plain tubes (tips)

Equipment for tempering (see pages 16–17)

Greaseproof (wax) paper piping bags (cones)

*1* Preheat the oven to 200°C (400°F) and line a heavy baking sheet with foil. For the choux pastry, put 250ml (8fl oz) boiling water into a heavy-based saucepan over a gentle heat. Add the butter to the water and bring slowly to the boil – the idea is to have the butter melted just when the water is about to boil. Sift the flour and the salt into a bowl.

*2* As soon as the butter and water mixture has come to the boil, remove it from the heat and sift in the flour immediately, beating hard with a wooden spoon or spatula until the mixture forms a ball and leaves the sides of the pan.

*Pipe out 36–40 bulbs of choux pastry onto a sheet of greaseproof (wax) paper.*

*Once cooked and cooled, make a hole in the choux balls in preparation for their filling.*

**3**  Transfer to a bowl and, using an electric whisk, beat in four eggs, one at a time. Mix for a minute, ensuring the bowl sides are scraped down. Transfer to a savoy bag with a 2cm (¾in) plain tube (tip) and pipe out 36–40 small bulbs onto the baking sheet. Bake for 30 minutes until the balls are well-risen and golden. Leave to cool, then use a knife to cut a hole in each.

**4**  For crème pâtissière to fill the choux balls, put the milk in a heavy-based saucepan over a gentle heat and bring to the boil. In a bowl, combine three eggs, the sugar and sifted cornflour – whisk until pale. Pour the boiling milk slowly over the egg mixture and whisk until combined. Return the mixture to the pan and bring back to the boil slowly, stirring until the mixture becomes a smooth custard. Sprinkle with sugar and cover with greaseproof (wax) paper to prevent a skin from forming. Leave to cool for 15 minutes and melt the dark chocolate. Uncover the custard and slowly stir in the melted dark chocolate. Leave to cool.

**5**  Whisk the cream until firm. Put half of the chocolate custard and half of the cream into two separate bowls. Using a hand whisk, blend through one third of the cream until it is half mixed into the custard. Repeat with the next third and finally the last portion, then mix until smooth. (Mixing as little as possible so as not to deflate the cream.) Place the mixture into a savoy bag fitted with a 1cm (½in) plain tube and pipe into the choux balls. Repeat with the remaining custard and cream. Once filled, place the choux balls (or profiteroles) on a tray and refrigerate.

*Pipe the fresh crème pâtissière into the choux balls and close the balls around their filling.*

*Dip the profiteroles into the tempered white chocolate and form a circle around the board.*

*Pile up the dipped balls to create a secure tower of white chocolate profiteroles.*

*6* Temper the white chocolate (see pages 146–147). Remove the profiteroles from the refrigerator and leave at room temperature for a few minutes. With the cake board in front of you, take a profiterole and dip a third of it into the white chocolate, removing any excess. Place in position about 4cm (1½in) in from the board edge, with the chocolate in contact with the board and facing inwards. Repeat the process to form a tight circle of profiteroles.

*7* Fill the circle in the centre with more dipped profiteroles. Then, start on the second layer, placing the balls about half their width in, to start making the cone shape. Once the second layer is complete, leave the chocolate to firm and then proceed with the third and fourth layers, decreasing the number in each layer as the circle becomes smaller. For stability, leave the chocolate to set every two or three layers. When the cone is complete, place in a cool place until required.

*8* To make the chocolate star decorations, place the remaining white chocolate into a greaseproof paper piping bag (cone). Copy the star template and place under greaseproof paper. Snip the end of the bag of chocolate and pipe around the outline – ten stars will be required. Leave them to dry, then spray with edible gold. Once dry, remove the stars from the paper and attach them to the pyramid using a little melted chocolate. Loop the ribbon to make a bow and secure with florist's wire. When twisted around the ribbon, the wire creates a spike to attach the bow to the Croquembouche.

*Serving Suggestions*

*This pyramid can be created in different sizes to accommodate the number of servings required. Traditionally, the bride and groom dismantle the pyramid placing one chou ball into the mouth of each guest. Other serving suggestions include:*

- *three profiteroles per person with warm chocolate sauce (see pages 146–147);*

- *two profiteroles per person with ice cream and warm chocolate sauce;*

- *two profiteroles per person with fresh raspberries and a blackberry coulis;*

- *two profiteroles per person with a warm fruit compôte of your choice.*

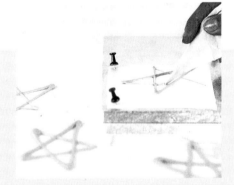

*Pipe over the the template onto greaseproof paper to achieve the star-shaped decorations.*

*Spray the stars with edible gold and attach to the profiterole tower with melted chocolate.*

*Secure the gold bow to the top of the tower using some florist's wire.*

The traditional taste combination of chocolate and coffee is celebrated in this delicious cake of contemporary design. The chocolate lattice pattern provides a delicate allure to the display and placing the cloches on glass cake plates creates a very modern, almost futuristic, effect.

# Cappuccino cloches

## CAKE AND DECORATION

15g (½oz) instant coffee

2.75kg (6lb) white ganache (see pages 142–145)

30cm (12in), 23cm (9in), 15cm (6in)
round chocolate cakes (see pages 138–139)

2.4kg (5lb) white marzipan

680g (1lb 8oz) milk chocolate paste
(see pages 148–149)

1.4kg (3lb) dark chocolate

## EQUIPMENT

Equipment for layering
and covering (see pages 18–20)

40cm (16in), 32cm (13in) and 25cm (10in)
circles of glass for stands

30cm (12in), 38cm (15in), 45cm (18in)
cardboard cake boxes

3 balloons

3 balloon ties

Equipment for tempering (see pages 16–17)

5cm (2in) round cutter

Greaseproof (wax) paper piping bags (cones)

*1* Place the coffee in a small cup and add just enough boiling water to dissolve it. Add the coffee mixture to the white ganache and mix thoroughly.

*2* Remove the skin from the top of the largest cake and slice through to form four thin layers of cake. Assemble by placing the base slice of cake onto a spare cake board. Add some of the ganache to the centre and spread towards the edge, leaving it thicker in the middle – this will help to form the dome shape. Place the next slice of cake on top and repeat the process with the ganache. Tuck down the edges of each slice of cake to reinforce

Fill the cake with the coffee ganache, piling up in the centre to create the dome shape.

Cover the top and sides of the cake with the coffee ganache, reinforcing the dome.

the dome shape. Repeat with the following two slices. Finish with a thin layer of ganache over the outside of the cake. Repeat for the remaining two cakes. Coat each dome with marzipan (see page 20) and leave to firm overnight.

*3* Using a palette knife, spread a coat of ganache over the marzipanned domes. With the end of the palette knife, create a 'swirl' pattern in the cream, repeating this all over each cake. Leave to firm overnight. Transfer each cake onto a glass circle (the best way to do this is to use two long knives to support the cakes).

*4* Prepare to create the cloches by first drawing a circle 5cm (2in) larger than each cake on the base of the cake boxes. Cut out these circles, giving three cake boxes with holes of 35cm (14in), 28cm (11in) and 20cm (8in). Blow up the balloons to fit snugly into these holes, securing with the balloon ties. These ties will later allow you to deflate the balloons easily.

*5* Roll out the chocolate paste to a thickness of about 5mm (¼in). Cut the paste into three strips 4cm (1½in) wide. These strips are to go around the bottom edges of each cloche, and should be 117cm (46in), 109cm (43in) and 66cm (26in) long. Take the 5cm (2in) round cutter and cut out half-circles along one edge on each strip – to a depth of 1.5cm (⅝in) – to form a crown or 'scalloped' effect. Roll up these strips ready for applying to the cloches.

*Liberally load the domes with coffee ganache, using a swirling action of the palette knife.*

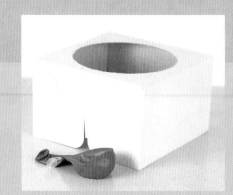

*Cut out circles in the cake boxes, slightly larger than the cakes, then blow up the balloons to fit.*

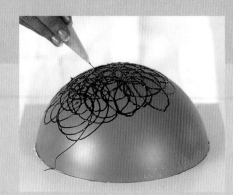

*Pipe spirals of chocolate over the surface of the balloons, making sure that all areas are covered.*

*6* Temper the dark chocolate (see pages 16–17), then place some of this dark chocolate into a greaseproof (wax) paper piping bag (cone) and cut a small hole in the end. Pipe chocolate over one of the balloons using a circular motion in order to create overlapping chocolate lines, working from the top of the balloon around and down. It is important to ensure that there are no large gaps in the chocolate lattice pattern as these could result in a weak spot when the chocolate is unsupported. While the chocolate is still wet, apply the crown strip around the base edge of the cloche, pressing it in place firmly. Place the cloche in the refrigerator for approximately 20 minutes so that it dries completely. Repeat this process to create the other cloches, using the remaining balloons.

*7* Remove the chocolate-covered balloons from the refrigerator with extreme care as the structure is still quite fragile. Release the balloon ties, gripping the balloons as a means of discharging the air very, very slowly. As long as the chocolate is well tempered, there should be no problems when deflating the balloons. When all the air has been expelled, the chocolate cloches will be held by their edges to their cake boxes. With a sharp knife and a steady hand, work around the cloches carefully to release them. Gently lift the cloches and place them over their corresponding cakes that are already sitting on their glass circles. The entire structure should be stable, but you can secure the cloches to the glass, if necessary, with a few dots of tempered chocolate.

*Fit the crown-like border around the base of the balloons while the piped chocolate is still wet.*

*Fit the cloches over their corresponding cakes, securing with melted chocolate if necessary.*

### Chocolate Tip

■ For an especially impressive effect, set the cakes onto three perspex or glass tubes at varying levels.

■ You could create three triangle lattice-piped pieces to form flat-sided pyramid-like cloches to fit over the cakes.

# Lattice ball and truffle centrepiece

This filigree case, enclosing delicious fresh cream truffles, will make a perfect accompaniment to the Cappuccino cloches (see pages 42–45). Place them as centrepieces on each table (with enough truffles for each guest) to bring a harmonious, themed look to your celebration. It also has immediate appeal as a decoration for the Christmas table. You could prepare the lattice ball using white chocolate and spray or paint it with gold or silver – perhaps with a red ribbon threaded through as though it were a bauble to hang from the Christmas tree.

This glorious chocolate centrepiece could also be entitled 'break in case of emergency', as the only way to get at the truffles is to break open its edible spherical cage. This recipe produces one centrepiece, but you can increase the quantities to make as many as you choose.

1 Temper the chocolate (see pages 16–17) and pour into a greaseproof (wax) paper piping bag (cone). Cut a small hole in the end of the bag and pipe thin lines of chocolate into the mould, using a circular motion. Overlap the spirals as they form and cover the entire surface of the half-sphere with chocolate lines. Finish the mould by piping an edge – a continuous line to join all the overlapped edges together. This is essential for the strength of the ball and also to create a surface for 'gluing' when you join the two halves to form the whole ball. Allow the chocolate to set and refrigerate for about 20 minutes, until it releases itself from the mould.

2 Prepare the chocolate truffles (see pages 50–53). If these centrepieces are being used at a wedding, it is a good idea to match the flavour of the truffle to the wedding cake. In this case, it would be cappuccino – a white chocolate ganache with a light coffee flavour (this can be enhanced with the addition of a little vanilla). Flavours for Christmas truffles include cherry brandy, advocaat or rum with cinnamon. The most important thing is that the flavour and the chocolate colour match the occasion.

### INGREDIENTS

115g (4oz) milk chocolate

12 truffles (see pages 50–53)

### EQUIPMENT

Equipment for tempering (see pages 16–17)

Greaseproof (wax) paper piping bags (cones)

15cm (6in) ball mould

3 Place the truffles into one half of the chocolate ball. Take a small amount of chocolate in a piping bag and carefully pipe around the edge to be joined. Sit the other half-sphere onto the chocolate line, ensuring that it is lined up evenly, then press into position gently, holding it in place while the chocolate starts to set. Handle with care as you put the ball on the table.

*Pipe overlapping spirals of chocolate into the mould, making sure that all areas are covered.*

*Place the truffles inside the half-sphere, being careful not to over-load.*

Pipe chocolate around the edge of the half-sphere, to join the two halves together.

Make sure that your latticed ball of truffles is dry and secure before you take it to the table.

### Chocolate Tip

For a wonderful multi-coloured lattice ball, use dark, milk and white chocolate piped randomly into the mould. The effect is very attractive and provides a range of chocolate flavours.

Assorted chocolate truffles make a wonderful gift for your guests. You can put them in beautiful boxes and lay them as place settings, or serve them up with coffee as an after-dinner treat. Why not decorate the boxes with coloured ribbon to tie in with the theme of your celebration?

# Truffle treats

## INGREDIENTS FOR 20 TRUFFLES

400g (14oz) ganache (see pages 142–143)

Flavouring of your choice, such as alcohol, tea, fruit tea, coffee or vanilla essence

150g (5¼oz) dark, milk or white chocolate

Coating of your choice, such as flaked chocolate, cocoa powder, icing (confectioner's) sugar, granulated sugar, flaked nuts, powdered nuts, croquant, or melted chocolate of a contrasting colour (to create a marbled effect)

## EQUIPMENT

Savoy bag

1cm (½in) plain tube (tip)

Equipment for tempering (see pages 16–17)

*1* As you are preparing the ganache (see pages 142–143), add a couple of drops of your chosen flavouring to it. Once the flavoured ganache is cold, place it in an airtight container and leave to stand overnight.

*2* Beat the ganache until it is smooth and slightly aerated. Place some into a savoy bag with a 1cm (½in) plain tube (tip) and pipe small bulbs of about 1.5cm (⅝in) in diameter onto a sheet of greaseproof (wax) paper. Leave them to firm at room temperature – 15°C (60°F) – for approximately two hours. (It is also possible to refrigerate the ganache bulbs for a short while if you wish to speed up the firming process.)

*Pipe out small bulbs of beaten ganache onto a sheet of greaseproof paper.*

*Once firm, roll the ganache between your fingers to create bite-sized balls.*

*3* Roll each firmed ganache bulb into a ball in your hands. Place the rolled balls back onto the greaseproof paper and leave them to firm once again for a short while.

*4* Temper the chocolate of your choice (see pages 16–17) and dip the finger ends of one hand into the tempered chocolate. Then, roll a ball of ganache in this same hand making sure that you cover the ganache ball with the chocolate completely. Place the chocolate-covered ball onto a clean sheet of greaseproof paper to allow it to dry. Repeat this dipping and covering process for all the remaining ganache balls and lay them out to dry – make sure that they are not touching each other or they will stick together as the chocolate sets.

*5* Once the first chocolate coating is dry, repeat the above process to give a second coat of chocolate to the truffles. Leave them to dry completely on a clean sheet of greaseproof paper at this stage if you are making plain truffles. If you wish to use coatings, roll the truffles in any of the suggested coatings to add texture and character. When you are rolling the truffles, make sure that they are entirely covered in their coatings and then lay them on a clean piece of greaseproof paper to dry thoroughly.

*6* Once the truffles are completely dry, you will need to store them in an airtight container at room temperature straight away. This recipe makes about 20 truffles, but you can up the quantities to make more and store them away for up to six weeks.

*Cover the ganache balls in tempered chocolate and leave to dry on greaseproof paper.*

*After a second coating of chocolate, you can cover the balls in the coating of your choice.*

*Make sure that the truffles are completely coated before setting them out to dry.*

## Rum truffle cakes

*These delightful little cakes are quite convenient as they help to use up the 'waste' from making a chocolate cake such as the Carnival cone (see pages 102–105) or Dark ruffles (see pages 116–119). The truffle cakes use both cake and chocolate off-cuts, but it is well worth baking a cake especially for the recipe.*

*1* Reduce the chocolate cake cuttings to fine crumbs, rubbing the pieces thoroughly between your fingers into a bowl.

*2* Place the chocolate-cake crumbs, apricot jam and rum into a large mixing bowl and stir together thoroughly.

*3* Melt the chocolate of your choice and quickly mix it through the cake-crumb mixture. The result should be a soft, pliable, slightly sticky paste. If the paste is too soft, add more cake crumbs. (A little adjustment is sometimes required according to the freshness of the cake crumbs that are being used.)

*4* Take pieces of approximately 30g (1oz) and form into ball shapes. Roll the balls in chocolate shavings or vermicelli (sprinkles) and place them into paper cases to serve.

**INGREDIENTS FOR 25 TRUFFLE CAKES**

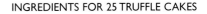

450g (1lb) chocolate cake cuttings

80g (3oz) apricot jam

60ml (2fl oz) rum

115g (4oz) dark, milk or white chocolate

170g (6oz) chocolate shavings
or chocolate vermicelli (sprinkles)

*Add the measure of rum to the chocolate cakecrumb and jam mixture.*

*Roll the mixture between your fingers to produce delicious bite-sized truffles.*

*Coat the truffles in chocolate shavings, so that they are completely covered.*

This is a striking four-tier stacked cake, simple in design with clean lines, bright chocolate and a hint of frivolity with gold stars and twisted willow. The combination of dark and white chocolate provides a most delicious double-edged domino delight.

# Domino effect

### CAKE AND DECORATION

30cm (12in), 23cm (9in), 15cm (6in) and 8cm (3in) round chocolate cakes (see pages 138–139)

30cm (12in), 23cm (9in), 15cm (6in) and 8cm (3in) round cake boards

2.1kg (4lb 8oz) ganache (see pages 142–145)

2.4kg (5lb) white marzipan

45cm (18in) round cake board for base

2.4kg (5lb) dark chocolate sauce (see pages 146–147)

450g (1lb) dark chocolate

1.4kg (3lb) white chocolate

30 strands artificial twisted willow

Florist's tape

Florist's gold spray

Gold confetti stars

Posy holder

Gold ribbon for board edge

### EQUIPMENT

Equipment for layering, covering and levelling (see pages 18–21)

7 cake dowels

Equipment for tempering (see pages 16–17)

8 sheets cellophane

Small sponge roller (as used for house painting)

Thin cotton gloves

Greaseproof (wax) paper piping bag (cone)

Comb scraper

*1* Layer the four cakes and cover each one with marzipan, including the edge of its corresponding cake board (see pages 18–20). Level the cakes (see page 21) and then leave them to dry for about 24 hours.

*2* Place the 30cm (12in) cake onto the 45cm (18in) round cake board and insert four cake dowels (see page 26). Insert three cake dowels into the 23cm (9in) cake, place it on top of the first cake, then place the third and top-tier cake in position. (Please note that cake dowels are not required for the third cake, as there is very little weight in the top cake.)

Use the roller to spread the tempered chocolate thinly over a sheet of cellophane.

Roll over the top sheet of cellophane, ironing out the chocolate inside.

*3* Warm the dark chocolate sauce to 35°C (95°F). Stand the stacked cakes on a turntable and place this on a baking sheet to catch any drips. Pour the sauce over the top cake, allowing it to cascade down over the three other tiers. Use a palette knife to ensure that the sauce is kept on course. Allow the chocolate sauce to firm and dry for about two hours. Carefully trim off any excess sauce from the base board edge, using a palette knife (this extra sauce can be reserved to use again).

*4* To make the domino pieces, temper the dark and white chocolate separately (see pages 16–17). Place two cellophane sheets onto your work surface. Pour a small amount of the tempered dark chocolate onto a piece of greaseproof (wax) paper, which should be placed right next to the cellophane, and spread the chocolate using a palette knife. Take the roller and load it by rolling it on the spread chocolate. Working quickly, roll the roller over the cellophane sheets to create a thin, mottled chocolate effect. Spread a 30cm (12in) x 38cm (15in) layer of white chocolate over the dark chocolate with a palette knife, then immediately place another piece of cellophane on top. Using a rolling pin, roll over the cellophane to form a very thin, flat sheet of chocolate. Using the rolling pin eliminates the risk of any air bubbles appearing. Place the chocolate sheets in the refrigerator for approximately 20 minutes. Repeat the above process until you produce three more chocolate sheets (this amount should be sufficient to produce the 80 dominoes required and will also allow for some eventual breakage).

*Cut out the domino pieces, releasing the chocolate from the cellophane sheets.*

*Use the comb scraper to scrape out individual lines of tempered white chocolate.*

*Roll up the strips of cellophane to form spirals of white chocolate.*

*5* Remove the sheets from the refrigerator one at a time. Place them on a clean, flat surface, mottled-side-down, removing the first sheet of cellophane by lifting a corner and peeling it back on itself with a quick, smooth action – thus ensuring an unmarked surface.

*6* Using a ruler and the point of a sharp knife, measure and mark notches 9cm (3½in) apart along one side and 4cm (1½in) apart along the adjacent side. Using a straight edge as a guide, use a sharp, thin-bladed knife to cut out the oblong pieces. This will release most pieces from the backing cellophane. If any stick, peel with a quick movement to preserve the shine. Handle the pieces with care, as they will mark easily – wear thin cotton gloves.

*7* Arrange the domino pieces around the cake, overlapping each one to show its white edge. Hold the pieces in place with a small amount of chocolate sauce applied from a piping bag (cone). Leave to dry overnight.

*8* To make the white curled pieces around the base board, take a strip of cellophane 5cm (2in) x 40cm (16in), spread it with tempered white chocolate and use a comb scraper to give individual lines of chocolate. Holding one end of the cellophane, firmly twist to form a spiral. Secure the ends onto a baking sheet with chocolate sauce and refrigerate for 20 minutes. Remove and arrange on the base board, wearing cotton gloves and using sauce as 'glue'.

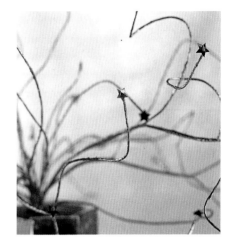

### Willow decoration

Artificial twisted willow is wire covered in a soft paper surface. Twist together the ends of 30 strands to form a firm short 'trunk' about 5cm (2in) in length. The ends protruding from this should be up to 30cm (12in) in length. Use florist's tape to bind around the trunk to give a firm hold.

Spray the twisted willow with florist's gold spray and leave to dry. Attach the gold confetti stars to the end of each wire with glue and leave to dry.

Insert a posy holder into the centre of the top tier, placing the wired willow trunk into this. Artistically bend and shape the wires to create the desired effect. Glue the ribbon around the base board.

*When the chocolate has set, unroll the cellophane strips to release the spirals.*

*Spray the twisted willow with gold spray and leave to dry before dressing the cake.*

# Almond rocher box centrepiece

This table centrepiece is designed to match the Domino effect cake (see pages 54–57), but could also be used at any occasion where sweets are required to be presented with a little imagination. These rochers are made with toasted strip (slivered) almonds and dark, milk and white chocolate, but you can use almost any kind of nut. You could even use truffles (see pages 50–53) if you prefer a smoother texture.

Whatever chocolate delicacies you choose to put inside, your guests will enjoy savouring the tasty treats and then devouring the gorgeous boxes. So, make sure that you make enough for everyone! This recipe produces one centrepiece, but you can up the quantities to make as many as you choose. You can vary the chocolate colours for alternative creations.

## INGREDIENTS

255g (9oz) white chocolate

200g (7oz) strip (slivered) almonds

50g (1¾oz) icing (confectioner's) sugar

60g (2oz) milk chocolate

## EQUIPMENT

Equipment for tempering (see pages 16–17)

Cellophane sheets

10cm (4 in) × 10cm (4 in), 10cm (4in) × 2.5cm (1in) and 2.5cm (1in) × 4cm (1½in) card templates

*1* Temper 200g (7oz) of the white chocolate (see pages 16–17) and pour onto a sheet of cellophane. Place a second sheet of cellophane on top and, using a rolling pin, spread the chocolate to create a very thin, even flat sheet. Place in the refrigerator for at least 20 minutes.

*2* Remove the chocolate sheets from the refrigerator and peel back one sheet of cellophane in a quick single action. Place the card templates onto the chocolate and, using a thin-bladed sharp knife or a craft knife, cut around the shapes. Each box will require one square shape (for the base), four larger oblongs (for the sides) and 12 smaller oblongs (for the stand-ups). If the cellophane does not peel away as each piece is cut, remove it by peeling quickly. Assemble the boxes, using a little tempered white chocolate to glue the pieces in place.

*3* Mix the strip (slivered) almonds with the icing (confectioner's) sugar. Toast the mixture under a grill, stirring 2–3 times during toasting. When the nuts are golden, remove them from the grill and allow to cool. Melt the milk and remaining white chocolate separately and mix half of the toasted nuts into each type of chocolate until coated. Spoon bite-sized piles of the chocolate–nut mixture onto greaseproof paper. Allow them to dry.

*4* Once the rochers are dry, place about 20 of them into each white chocolate box and distribute them as centrepieces on the tables.

*Roll out the tempered chocolate between cellophane sheets, so that it is thin and flat.*

*Cut out the domino shapes and peel away the cellophane if it continues to stick.*

*Erect the box, attaching the domino pieces with a little tempered chocolate.*

## Variation

*You can put any kind of sweet into the box, depending on your preferences, for example:*

Pipe small discs of dark, milk or white chocolate onto a sheet of greaseproof (wax) paper. While the chocolate is still soft, press in some nuts or glacé fruits. Try hazelnuts, walnuts, almonds, glacé cherries or crystallized ginger. Leave to dry so that the pieces set firmly into the chocolate.

Lay out the chocolate-covered nuts on greaseproof paper to dry.

Stack the domino box with the almond rochers, ready to take to the table.

*This elaborate-looking dark chocolate pyramid, embellished with gold, contains a moist chocolate cake richer than the treasures of Egypt. It is much easier to prepare than it looks and will leave your guests in awe. Serve with warm, dark chocolate sauce for a further touch of decadence.*

# Kemet pyramid

## CAKE AND DECORATION

35 x 35 x 8cm (14 x 14 x 3in)
square chocolate cake (see pages 138–139)

2.4kg (5lb) ganache (see pages 142–145)

2.75kg (6lb) white marzipan

25 x 25 x 13cm (10 x 10 x 5 in)
square chocolate cake (see pages 138–139)

45cm (18in) and 25cm (10in) square cake boards

2.4kg (5lb) dark chocolate sauce (see pages 146–147)

Gold ribbon for board edge

## FOR THE CAKE ACCESSORIES

1.75kg (3lb 10oz) dark chocolate paste
(see pages 148–149)

Edible gold spray or paint

900g (2lb) dark chocolate

## EQUIPMENT

Equipment for layering, covering
and levelling (see pages 18–21)

9cm (3½in) ball mould

Spirit level

Triangle and cartouche templates
(see pages 152–155)

Small, soft paintbrush

5mm (¼in) sugarpaste ribbon strip cutter

**1** To prepare the bottom tier of cake, slice the larger chocolate cake horizontally into layers and sandwich with ganache. On the top, mark 2.5cm (1in) in all the way around to draw a 30cm (12in) square. Cut at an angle, using the marked line as a starting point and cut down to the outside edge, forming a slope. Place the cake on its board and spread ganache all over.

**2** Roll out a 1.6kg (3lb 8oz) piece of marzipan to cover the cake in one single piece. Place the marzipan over the cake, using a cake smoother to obtain a smooth, flat top and sides. Trim off the excess marzipan, level (see page 21) and leave the cake to stand for 24 hours.

*For the top cake, the stack of cake layers in half on a diagonal, steadying them as you do so.*

*Join the pieces to form a roof shape, then slice though to create the pyramid.*

## Cake Accessories

**To make the triangles:**

Knead the chocolate paste, then roll it out to a 1.5cm (⅝in) thickness using a little icing (confectioner's) sugar for dusting. Cut out 28 triangular pieces, referring to the triangle template. Leave them to stand overnight to allow them to firm. Turn the pieces over and, using a craft knife, score 6 equally spaced parallel lines across 14 of the triangles and 6 vertical lines on the remaining 14 triangles. Using a sharp, thin-bladed knife, cut a V-shape between the scored lines, to half the depth of the piece. To eliminate rough edges, use a paintbrush dipped in water. Leave for 24 hours, then spray with edible gold.

*3* For the top tier, slice the smaller cake horizontally into layers and sandwich with ganache. Cut diagonally across the 25 × 13cm (10 × 5in) side. Using ganache, join the two long sides together to form a 'roof' shape. Place on the 25cm (10in) cake board.

*4* Mark the centre point on the apex (or roof ridgeline), and cut a diagonal down to the cake board edge. Repeat on the opposite side to form the four-sided pyramid. Discard the waste cake pieces or keep to make Rum truffle cakes (see page 53). Coat with ganache.

*5* To cover the pyramid, roll out the remaining marzipan quite thinly, but so that it is large enough to cover both the cake and the cake board edge in one piece. Place the marzipan over the cake and use a cake smoother in order to create smooth, flat sides. Trim off the excess marzipan and moisten the board edge with a little water to secure the marzipan. Allow 24 hours to dry.

*6* Warm the dark chocolate sauce to around 35°C (95°F) (see pages 146–147) and pour over the cakes, paddling with a palette knife to create an even coat. Tap the cakes on their boards to help remove air bubbles. If bubbles persist, pop them with a pin while the sauce is still in its flowing state. Do not try to clean away the drips at this time. Leave to dry overnight then, using the back of a knife, clean away excess sauce from the board edges.

*Cut V-shapes into the chocolate paste triangles and leave them to dry.*

*Make sure that the marzipan covering the pyramid is perfectly flat and smooth.*

*Pour the dark chocolate over the top of the pyramid, allowing it to slide down the sides.*

*7* Using a glue stick, trim the base board edge with the gold ribbon. Put the triangle pieces (see *Cake Accessories*) in place around the bottom-tier cake. Ensure that there is even spacing between each piece. Fasten the triangles to the cake using a little chocolate sauce as the glue, pressing firmly to adhere.

*8* Using a small amount of chocolate sauce as glue, place the gold chocolate balls (see *Cake Accessories*) on the base tier, setting them about 8cm (3in) in from the corners and ensuring that they are equally aligned with each other. Place a spare cake board on top of the balls and check that it is level using a spirit level. Apply gentle pressure to achieve a flat surface.

*9* Fix the cartouche pieces (see *Cake Accessories*) to the pyramid top tier, using a little chocolate sauce as glue. Press firmly into position. Allow to dry and set set overnight before assembling the cakes. To transport this cake to the celebration venue, pack the two cake tiers into separate boxes and assemble the structure on site.

accessories

*Use a palette knife to cover all sides of the pyramid with a layer of chocolate sauce.*

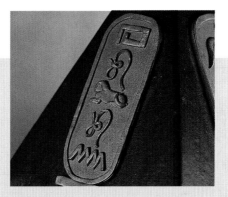

*Use chocolate sauce to attach the cartouche pieces to the sides of the pyramid.*

**To make the golden balls:**

Make four chocolate balls using a solid ball mould (see page 15). Put some tempered chocolate (see pages 16–17) on your hands and roll the balls to add texture. Dry on greaseproof paper and spray gold.

**To make the cartouches:**

Roll out the remaining chocolate paste to a 5mm (¼in) thickness. Cut out four cartouche shapes with a sharp craft knife. Roll out the remaining paste to a 3mm (⅛in) thickness. Using the ribbon strip cutter, cut four strips and set aside. Also cut out the hieroglyphs, referring to the templates to trace onto greaseproof paper the letters of the names of the bride and groom. Moisten the strips and press them to the edge of the cartouches. Use a smoother to achieve a flat, even surface. Apply the hieroglyphs to the cartouches in the same way. Leave to dry for 24 hours, then spray with edible gold.

*Moisten the strips of chocolate paste before attaching them to the cartouche edges.*

*Traditional wedding cakes were made with royal icing. The fashion was simple scrolls and shells — perhaps with the addition of small sugar roses, silver horseshoes and wedding rings. Here we give tradition a modern twist, using rich piped chocolate and shiny silver balls.*

# Pipes and scrolls

### CAKE AND DECORATION

25cm (10in), 20cm (8in) and 15cm (6in) square chocolate cakes (see pages 138–139)

680g (1lb 8oz) apricot jam

680g (1lb 8oz) ganache (see pages 142–145)

35cm (14in), 30cm (12in) and 25cm (10in) square cake boards

1.8kg (4lb) white marzipan

2.25kg (5lb) chocolate fudge icing (see page 151)

170g (6oz) cooking chocolate

9 glass test tubes

225g (8oz) silver balls

Curly silver ting ting (like twisted willow)

Icing (confectioner's) sugar for dusting

### EQUIPMENT

Equipment for layering, covering and levelling (see pages 18–21)

Comb scraper

Greaseproof (wax) paper for piping bags (cones)

Number 44 star piping tube (tip)

Petal piping tube

Number 3 plain piping tube

Apple corer

Cocktail stick (toothpick)

*1* Layer the cakes (see pages 18–19), sandwiching each with one layer of apricot jam and two layers of ganache, then place each cake onto its corresponding cake board. Add a thin coat of apricot jam to the outside of each cake to finish the layering process and provide the glue for the marzipan. Roll out the marzipan thinly and cover each cake with one continuous piece, using a cake smoother to even the top and sides. Trim off the excess marzipan and leave for 24 hours.

*2* Prepare the chocolate fudge icing (see page 151), being careful not to over-beat as this can incorporate too much air and cause problems with bubbles when coating the cakes. Using a

*Use a comb scraper to add lines of texture to the fudge icing on the sides of the cakes.*

*Smooth the fudge icing on the top of the cakes, using a straight edge, and trim off any excess.*

palette knife, coat the sides of each cake and finish with a comb scraper to give the characteristic ridged sides. Coat the top of each cake as well and smooth flat, using a straight edge. Coat the cake board edges using a palette knife held at an angle to remove any excess fudge icing. Allow the fudge to dry overnight (or for at least six hours) before proceeding onto the following steps.

*3* The 25cm (10in) cake will have four scrolls to each top edge, the 20cm (8in) cake will have three scrolls and the 15cm (6in) cake will have two. Using a small knife mark these divisions to indicate where piping should start and finish. Place the number 44 star tube (tip) into a piping bag (cone), fill the bag with chocolate fudge and pipe the first S-shaped scrolls around the cake tops. Then pipe a second smaller scroll next to each first scroll. Repeat these double S-shaped scrolls on the base board around the edges of the cakes.

*4* Over-pipe the scrolls using a petal tube and the same piping action, then, using the number 44 tube, pipe an edging of shells around the top edge of the cakes. Pipe the single line-work outline on the top of the cake and on the board, using a number 3 plain tube.

*5* On the two bottom tiers, measure 2.5cm (1in) in from the corner line-work, on imaginary diagonal lines, and make a small mark. These marks will be the positions for the cake pillars.

*Use an apple corer to remove tubes of cake in preparation for the test tubes.*

*Pipe out the succulent scrolls of chocolate fudge around the edges of the cakes.*

*Fill the test tubes unevenly with the silver balls — use as many or as little as you choose.*

Use the apple corer to remove a plug of cake at these specific points, ensuring that you leave a clean hole through to the cake board. Make one single hole in the centre of the top-tier cake.

*6* Melt the cooking chocolate, transfer to a piping bag, then fill each hole to within 2cm (³/₄in) of the top. For greater precision, measure 2cm (³/₄in) along a cocktail stick and mark with a pen. Use the cocktail stick as a dipstick as a means of checking the level. When set, this chocolate plug is to be the support for the test tube pillar. Insert all four test tubes just before the chocolate sets completely. Place a spare cake board on top of the four tubes and test that it is straight using a spirit level.

*7* Using a piping bag (cone) with a hole cut in the end, pour silver balls into the test tubes – fill to different levels according to your preference. Scatter a few balls onto the cake tops and onto the cake boards as well, to create a random effect. Build up the second layer, inserting the next four test tubes and adding the silver balls.

*8* Insert the final test tube into the centre of the top-tier cake. Part-fill with silver balls and arrange silver ting ting on the top. Dust the finished cake lightly with icing (confectioner's) sugar or cocoa powder for a different effect.

*Make sure that the test tubes are completely level, in preparation for the next cake.*

*Dust the cake with icing (confectioner's) sugar or cocoa powder for a different look.*

# Textures and curls

The flexibility of chocolate means that it can be used to create a variety of edible decorative pieces that both look stylish and taste good. Melted chocolate can be manipulated into a range of unusual shapes, adding interest to any cake. Over half of the cakes in this book contain some form of chocolate decoration that is made separately from the main cake, then placed into position. You can use different colours of chocolate as a means of creating the effect of your choice – experiment!

You can choose from curls (see page 24) – caramel, candy-striped, coloured or brushed with gold; short curls, loose like pencil shavings, spiralling or scraped or grated from a block of chocolate; ruffles; flat piped pieces – snowflakes and stars; textured curved shapes created on plastics and paper; hollow spheres – both solid and filigree; mottled chocolate shaped in moulds; cut shapes using a knife and templates; lattice domes; roses; draped chocolate to look like soft fabric and flat sheets of chocolate.

The possibility of using these delicious decorations is not limited to the cakes with which they are shown in this book. Many of them would make fabulous adornments for simple desserts and puddings – particularly ice creams and bombes. Your dinner parties will never be the same again!

*This pretty floral cake is bright and fresh – ideal for a spring wedding or celebration. The cake is covered with white chocolate paste tinted green, giving it a verdant quality. Smooth surfaces form a backdrop for the sugar flowers grouped together and interspersed with chocolate paste pebbles.*

# Spring wedding

### CAKE AND DECORATION

25cm (10in) oval and 15cm (6in) round chocolate cakes (see pages 138–139)

900g (2lb) ganache (see pages 142–145)

1.25kg (2lb 12oz) white marzipan

40cm (16in) oval and 15cm (6in) round cake boards

1.4kg (3lb) white chocolate paste (see pages 146–147)

Mint green paste food colouring

Icing (confectioner's) sugar for dusting

30ml (1fl oz) clear alcohol

Peach food colouring

60g (2oz) confectioner's varnish

Sugar flowers as required

Ribbon for board edge

### EQUIPMENT

Equipment for layering, covering and levelling (see pages 18–21)

Pasta-rolling machine (optional)

3 cake dowels

Small, soft paintbrush or aerograph pen

*1* Layer the cakes, fill and coat with ganache and cover with marzipan (see pages 18–20). Place the cakes on their corresponding cake boards and level (see page 21).

*2* Put aside 60g (2oz) of white chocolate paste and colour the remainder green. When the colour is partly mixed in, pass through pasta rollers to obtain a smooth paste. Roll it out, using a little icing (confectioner's) sugar to dust with. Moisten the marzipan with alcohol using the paintbrush, then cover the round cake with the paste, starting on the top, and working around and down the side. Trim off excess paste and polish with the flat of your hand. Coat the oval cake and the top of the base board in the same way. Leave to dry overnight. Insert three dowels into the base cake (see page 26). Place the round cake off-centre on the base cake.

*3* Make the pebbles by breaking off small pieces of white chocolate paste and rolling them between your fingers and thumb to form the desired shapes (use a little icing sugar to prevent sticking to your hands). Leave them to dry overnight. Add peach food colouring to the pebbles, either by dabbing with a small, soft brush or spraying lightly with an aerograph pen to create a speckled effect. Leave to dry for 24 hours, then coat with confectioner's varnish for extra shine.

*4* The miniature flowers used here are daffodils, bluebells, snowdrops, primroses and violets as well as an assortment of leaves. The top flowers are arranged in a tiny block of dry-foam covered in sphagnum moss. The side sprays are wired and taped. Position the flowers and the pebbles, securing with chocolate. Trim the base board edge with a ribbon.

*A simple, no-nonsense cake with beautiful fresh flowers used as the only decoration. For a wedding occasion, these flowers could mirror the bride's bouquet – in variety, colour and style. You can use a number of different arrangements – all of which will look superb in their own, unique way.*

# Summer wedding

## CAKE AND DECORATION

25cm (10in) round chocolate cake (see pages 138–139)

35cm (14in) round cake board

680g (1lb 8oz) dark chocolate ganache (see pages 142–145)

450g (1lb) white marzipan

680g (1lb 8oz) milk chocolate

40ml (1½fl oz) pure corn oil

60ml (2fl oz) confectioner's varnish

Ribbon for board edge

Ribbon for around cake, if required

Fresh flowers, as required

Oasis

10cm (4in) plastic dish

## EQUIPMENT

Equipment for layering, covering and levelling (see pages 18–21)

Equipment for tempering (see pages 16–17)

Small, soft paintbrush (preferably camel hair)

*1* Layer the cake, fill and coat with ganache, then cover with marzipan (see pages 18–20). Level (see page 21) and leave overnight to allow the cake to firm.

*2* Temper the milk chocolate (see pages 16–17), add the corn oil and mix well, trying not to incorporate too much air while stirring, as this will result in a problem with air bubbles when coating the cake. Pour the tempered chocolate over the cake, allowing it to flow around and down the sides, also covering the cake board. Use a palette knife to ease the chocolate into the right direction. If any air bubbles rise to the surface, prick these with a pin while the chocolate is still very fluid, so that no marks are left. Leave the cake to dry at room temperature for a couple of hours.

*3* Using a soft brush, apply the confectioner's varnish to the cake in long, smooth strokes – start at the top and work your way down and around, also covering the chocolate-covered board. Leave to dry and harden for 24 hours. (This period of time is also required to allow the alcohol fumes in the varnish to disappear.)

*4* Apply a ribbon to the base board edge, sticking it in place with a glue stick. The smooth, rounded and glossy surface of this cake, however, will look good with or without a ribbon. The fresh flowers for the top of this cake are arranged in Oasis on a flat plastic dish. Place them into position as late as possible on the day of the wedding.

## Arrangement variations

You can choose different flower arrangements for the top of your cake to reflect the feel of the wedding or celebration. The off-beat arrangement below would suit an exotic, tropical party or perhaps prepare a bride and groom for a sun-drenched honeymoon. The tower of flowers on the right, however – featuring stunning red roses woven with vibrant ivy leaves – would be fitting for a more formal romantic affair.

You could also scatter the cake board with fresh flower petals to obtain a random confetti feel. (Make sure that you do this just before serving, however, as single petals wilt quickly.)

### Flower Tip

Ensure that your flowers remain fresh throughout your celebration, by keeping them cool until you are ready to place the arrangement on the cake.

To keep the surface of your cake intact, you could put the plastic dish containing your flowers onto a thin cake board before placing it in position.

*This tower of rich, dark, glossy chocolate is brought to life with colourful marzipan horse chestnuts and soft, silk autumnal leaves – creating a strikingly detailed but wonderfully mellow seasonal cake. Your guests will definitely be dazzled by this unusual and evocative creation.*

# Autumn wedding

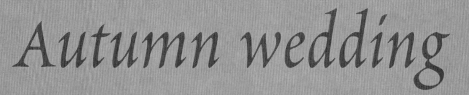

### CAKE AND DECORATION

35cm (14in), 23cm (9in), 15cm (6in) and 8cm (3in) chocolate cakes (see pages 138–139)

1.8kg (4lb) ganache (see pages 142–145)

2.4kg (5lb) white marzipan

35cm (14in), 23cm (9in), 15cm (6in) and 8cm (3in) round cake boards

45cm (18in) round base board

2.75kg (6lb) dark chocolate sauce (see pages 146–147)

Ribbon to trim base board edge

130g (4½oz) milk chocolate paste (see pages 148–149)

170g (6oz) white marzipan

285g (10oz) pale green marzipan

30ml (1fl oz) confectioner's varnish

Brown food colouring

16 silk leaves in autumn shades

### EQUIPMENT

Equipment for layering, covering and levelling (see pages 18–21)

8 cake dowels

5cm (2in) round cutter

Small, soft sponge (soaked in water)

Small, soft paintbrush

1  Layer the four chocolate cakes, fill and coat with ganache, then cover them with a layer of white marzipan (see pages 18–20). Allow the four cakes to firm, then place them on their corresponding round cake boards and level (see page 21).

2  Strengthen the two round base cakes with cake dowels (see page 26) and stack all four chocolate cakes together. It is preferable to place the top three cakes in a slightly off-centre position, to provide a generous ledge for the decorative chocolate and marzipan horse chestnuts to rest upon.

*Pour the warm dark chocolate sauce over the cakes, so that they are coated all over.*

*Paint the horse chestnut centres with confectioner's varnish to give them a glow.*

*3* Place the stacked cakes onto a turntable, and stand this on a baking sheet in order to catch any drips. Warm the prepared dark chocolate sauce to about 35°C (95°F) and pour gently over the four cakes. Allow the chocolate sauce to flow down and coat all four cakes evenly. Leave the structure to dry overnight.

*4* Remove any excess chocolate sauce from the base board edge using a palette knife. Using a glue stick, attach a matching ribbon to trim the base board edge.

*5* To make the horse chestnuts, start by cutting out the chocolate paste into 12 equal pieces. Roll each chocolate piece into a small ball and leave all the balls to dry overnight. Once they are dry, paint the chocolate balls with confectioner's varnish in order to provide some extra shine. Leave the balls to dry for at least four hours.

*6* Roll out the white marzipan to a thickness of 5mm (¼in) and cut out 12 circles of 5cm (2in) in diameter. Repeat this process with the green marzipan. Place a green disc on top of a white one and cut in half with a sharp knife.

*7* Pick up a chocolate paste ball, which is to be the centre of each chestnut, and place a two-tone half disc (white side against the chocolate) onto it. Place the other half disc on the

*Put the discs of green and white marzipan together and cut them in half.*

*You can assemble the horse chestnuts in degrees of maturity, exposing more or less of the centres.*

opposite side of the chocolate ball in order to create an 'open mouth'. With great care, mould the marzipan around the chocolate ball. Place the marzipan balls on a spare cake board.

*8* To create the spines on the horse chestnuts, roll out a 5g (⅛-oz) piece of green marzipan into a 'sausage' shape and cut into 20 equal pieces. Roll each piece into a ball and, with your index finger against the palm of your other hand, mould each marzipan ball into a point at one end. Attach each spine to the chestnut case with a little moisture by dabbing the end of the spine against a wet sponge. Leave the finished marzipan chestnuts to dry overnight. Spray or brush with a little brown food colouring to add texture.

*9* Fix the chestnuts onto the cake, securing them with a little chocolate sauce. Place the silk autumn leaves in position to complete the arrangement. If you wish to enhance the shine on the finished cake, this can be achieved by using a thin coat of edible confectioner's varnish applied with a soft paintbrush.

horse chestnut

*Attach the spines to the marzipan jackets, by moistening them with a damp sponge.*

*Place the finished horse chestnuts on the cake ledges, using a little chocolate sauce.*

# Leaf and chestnut centrepiece

This table centrepiece complements the Autumn wedding or celebration cake beautifully (see pages 78–81), with its shiny dark chocolate finish and delicious chocolate and marzipan chestnuts. You can create the leaf in whatever size you like, to hold the required amount of chocolates.

It is possible to alter the shape of the leaf dish to reflect the theme of your celebration. A maple leaf, for example, would be perfect to convey a Canadian influence, or you could use a tropical leaf to provide a little exoticism to the occasion. In this particular recipe, the chocolate dish is fashioned in an oak-leaf shape. This recipe produces one centrepiece, but you can up the quantities to make as many of them as you choose.

## INGREDIENTS

1.8kg (4lb) sugarpaste (rolled fondant)
(see page 150)

250g (9oz) dark chocolate

10 horse chestnuts (see pages 80–81)

Silk autumn leaves (optional)

## EQUIPMENT

Leaf-shaped template (see pages 152–155)

Equipment for tempering (see pages 16–17)

Small, soft paintbrush

*1* Knead 900g (2lb) of the sugarpaste (rolled fondant) until it is pliable and roll it out to fit the template. Leave it quite thick – about 5cm (2in). Put the template in position and cut around the shape, removing any excess sugarpaste. Use your fingers to mould the piece and create rounded corners. If required, cut away any further detail.

*2* Wrap the piece of sugarpaste in foil and place it on a spare cake board. Knead the remaining sugarpaste until it is pliable and roll it out until it is large enough to fit over the wrapped shape. Drape over and press into position in order to create a mould. Allow to dry for at least 24 hours.

*3* Place a cake board on top of the sugarpaste and flip it over so that the foil-wrapped piece of paste is visible. Remove this piece carefully, ensuring not to damage the new mould. Allow at least another 48 hours drying time for the mould.

*4* Line the inside of the mould with foil, smoothing it down as much as possible. Temper the chocolate (see pages 16–17) and use a small paintbrush to paint four layers of chocolate onto the foil – allowing drying time between each layer. Place in the refrigerator for 30 minutes, then remove, lift out of the mould and carefully peel away the foil from the chocolate to reveal the leaf-shaped chocolate dish. (You can put aside the sugarpaste to be used another time.)

*Cut around the leaf-shaped template to produce a thick leaf of sugarpaste.*

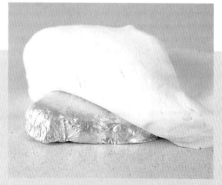

*Mould the sugarpaste (rolled fondant) around the foil leaf shape.*

5 Arrange the horse chestnuts in the leaf dish, adding a few silk autumn leaves sparingly into the leaf dish to create a slight contrast in the brown overtone. Distribute the dish as a centrepiece on the table.

## Variations

■ The method used here to create a simple dish shape, lends itself well to making any simple form. You could, for example, create a star shape, a crescent moon or a triangle.

■ Other marzipan shapes, such as acorns and pine cones would also look great in this autumnal chocolate dish.

■ Or an alternative centre for the horse chestnut is a small ganache truffle.

Coat the inside of the mould (over the foil) with tempered chocolate and allow to dry.

Assemble the marzipan horse chestnuts, ready for loading into the chocolate leaf.

*The inspiration for this dramatic single-tier cake is crisp winter snow. Virginal white chocolate paste and white chocolate are the sweet mediums used to create this pure, angelic cake, with beautifully detailed chocolate snowflakes and snowballs as the edible winter decorations.*

# Winter wedding

## CAKE AND DECORATION

28cm (11in) and 32cm (13in)
eight-sided cake boards

23cm (9in) eight-sided chocolate
cake (see pages 138–139)

450g (1lb) ganache (see pages 142–145)

680g (1lb 8oz) white marzipan

60g (2oz) icing (confectioner's) sugar,
plus extra for dusting

900g (2lb) white chocolate paste
(see pages 148–149)

15ml (½fl oz) clear alcohol

450g (1lb) white chocolate

Disco violet dust (see pages 156–157)

## EQUIPMENT

Hot glue gun

Equipment for layering, covering
and levelling (see pages 18–21)

Small, soft paintbrush

3 different sized half-ball moulds

Equipment for tempering (see pages 16–17)

Greaseproof (wax) paper piping bags (cones)

Template for snowflakes – three sizes
(see pages 156–157)

*1* Glue the cake boards together, centring the small board on the large one. Layer the cake, fill and coat with ganache, then cover with marzipan (see pages 18–20) and level (see page 21).

*2* Roll out the white chocolate paste using a little icing (confectioner's) sugar to dust. Brush the marzipan with alcohol to ensure good adhesion, then cover with the paste.

*3* Use a cake smoother to give an even finish, then trim off the excess paste around the edge. Roll out the remaining paste and cover the board steps, using a cake smoother to level.

*Make sure that the cake is smoothly covered with marzipan, but that the sides are angular.*

*Cover the cake with chocolate paste, with a portion extending over the cake boards as steps.*

**4** To make the snowballs, you will need to use three different-sized, half-ball moulds. Temper the white chocolate (see pages 16–17) and place some in a greaseproof (wax) paper piping bag (cone). Make a small hole in the end and pipe into the half-ball moulds in a circular fashion, ensuring that the circles are overlapping and that there are no large gaps. Place the moulds in the refrigerator for at least 15 minutes.

**5** Take the chocolate halves out of the moulds and stick two of them together with a little tempered chocolate to form a sphere. Create a bond of tempered chocolate around the edge and hold the two halves in place until they are fully secure.

**6** To make the snowflakes, place a piece of cellophane over the snowflake templates and pipe with the white chocolate to produce three different sizes of snowflakes (four of each size are required for this cake). Leave the snowflakes to dry and then place them in the refrigerator for at least 20 minutes.

**7** Fix the white snowflakes and snowballs in position, securing them with tempered white chocolate. Put the icing sugar into a sieve and dust the entire cake liberally to mimic a light snowfall. A wonderfully festive effect can be achieved by sprinkling with disco violet dust to add a sparkle to the finished cake.

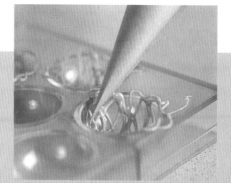

*Pipe some tempered white chocolate into different sized moulds, overlapping the spirals.*

*Bond two halves together with chocolate to form filigree snowball shapes.*

## Variation

*While this particular cake is produced entirely in white chocolate, an equally stunning effect can be created by using dark chocolate and dusting the finished cake with icing sugar in order to achieve the snow-covered look.*

Pipe out the snowflake shapes in tempered white chocolate, using the templates.

Assemble the balls and flakes on the cake and sprinkle with icing (confectioner's) sugar.

*This luxurious combination of cherry and chocolate, adorned with its delicate lattice of dark chocolate, is liberally laced with alcohol to give a distinct sophisticated appeal. A deliciously decadent dessert with a real kick, this celebratory cake is definitely not for the faint-hearted.*

# Kir royal

## CAKE AND DECORATION

25cm (10in) round chocolate cake (see pages 138–139)

450g (1lb) dark chocolate

35cm (14in) cake board

125ml (4fl oz) kirsch

1 litre (32fl oz) fresh whipping cream

450g (1lb) Amarino cherries
(black cherries soaked in brandy)

## EQUIPMENT

Equipment for layering (see pages 18–19)

Equipment for tempering (see pages 16–17)

Pastry brush

Cellophane strip 2cm (¾in) taller than
the layered cake, and as long as its circumference

Greaseproof (wax) paper piping bags (cones)

20cm (8in) cardboard cake box

1 balloon

1 balloon tie

Absorbent paper

*1* Cut the cake into layers (see pages 18–19) and coat the base with a thin layer of tempered dark chocolate (see pages 16–17). When set, the chocolate forms a firm base. Place this layer (chocolate-side-down) onto the cake board and brush with kirsch to moisten the sponge.

*2* Whisk the cream until firm and spread 200ml (7fl oz) onto the sponge with a palette knife.

*3* Put the next sponge layer in place, brush with kirsch, then spread another 200ml (7fl oz) of cream. Take 80g (3oz) of the Amarino cherries and chop, using a sharp knife, to create a pulp.

*Coat the base layer of cake with tempered dark chocolate, spreading right to the edge.*

*After moistening with kirsch, spread the whisked cream thickly onto the cake.*

Spread two thirds of the cherry pulp onto the cream layer, mixing in slightly to create a cherry–pink colour (reserve the other third for later).

**4** Put the third sponge layer into position. Brush with kirsch and, again, spread with 200ml (7fl oz) of cream and level to the edges. Place the fourth sponge layer into position on top of the cream and brush liberally with kirsch.

**5** Use the remaining cream to coat the top and sides of the cake. Ensure a smooth even surface with no cake showing through. Apply the reserved cherry pulp sparingly, using a palette knife, a little at a time, over the entire cake – blending with the cream to create a mottled effect. Place in the refrigerator while you are preparing the chocolate for the next stage.

**6** Lay the strip of cellophane flat on the work surface. Place some tempered dark chocolate in a greaseproof (wax) paper piping bag (cone) and cut the end to create a small hole. Pipe criss-crossed diagonal lines over the strip, creating a lattice pattern. Ensure the chocolate piping spills over on to the work surface at both sides of the strip. Lift the cellophane while the chocolate is still wet and apply it to the cake, pressing the chocolate against the cream. Ensure that the strip is level with the cake base and push firmly into position. Leave the cellophane attached to that cake and refrigerate for about 15 minutes.

*Lay the second layer of cake onto the cream and moisten with kirsch.*

*The central layer of cream needs to be spread liberally with cherry pulp.*

*The cherry pulp will blend with the cream coating, creating a mottled effect.*

7  Cut a 15cm (6in) hole in the cake box base. Blow up the balloon to fit snugly into this hole, close the balloon with a tie to enable it to be deflated easily. Place some more tempered dark chocolate into a greaseproof paper piping bag, cut a small hole in the end and pipe in a circular motion over the inflated balloon. Start at the top and work your way around and down, ensuring even coverage and leaving no large areas without chocolate (see pages 44–45). It is advisable to pipe an edge around the balloon, level with the cake box – this ensures a strong rim to the chocolate bowl. Refrigerate for 20 minutes.

8  Remove the box and the chocolate-piped balloon from the refrigerator. Slowly deflate the balloon, ensuring an even release from the chocolate. When the balloon is completely removed, the chocolate bowl may still be attached to the cake box. Gently ease the bowl away from the box by sliding a sharp knife between them – take great care, as the chocolate is very fragile.

9  Drain the remaining amarino cherries on absorbent paper. Remove the cake from the refrigerator and gently peel away the cellophane from around the cake, leaving the chocolate-trellis decoration standing proudly around the cake top and sides.

10  Place the chocolate bowl in the centre of the cake top, tilting slightly. Group some of the drained cherries around the base board and the remainder in the chocolate basket on the top.

*Serving Suggestion*

*This cake is simply delicious when it is served with a portion of juicy Amarino cherries on the side.*

Pipe thin, criss-crossed lines of tempered dark chocolate onto cellophane.

Holding the cellophane edge, press the chocolate lattice around the cake.

When the chocolate is dry, use great care to remove the cellophane strip.

*The chocolate and orange taste combination is possibly one of the best marriages of flavour there is. In this recipe the moist orange cake is accompanied by marzipan, coated in milk and dark chocolate. Use sugar or artificial orange blossoms and oranges for decoration.*

# Orange domes

### CAKE AND DECORATION

30cm (12in), 23cm (9in) and 15cm (6in) round orange cakes (see pages 138–139)

40cm (16in), 32cm (13in) and 25cm (10in) round cake boards

1.8kg (4lb) ganache (see pages 142–145)

2.4kg (5lb) white marzipan

2.4kg (5lb) milk chocolate paste (see pages 148–149)

60ml (2fl oz) clear alcohol

680g (1lb 8oz) dark chocolate sauce (see pages 146–147)

Gold-edged ribbon for board edges

Sugar orange-blossom flowers

Dark green leaves

Sugar oranges

### EQUIPMENT

Equipment for layering and covering (see pages 18–20)

Pastry brush

Food grater

Greaseproof (wax) paper piping bags (cones)

Hot glue gun

Ribbon cutter wheel

Airbrush or small, soft paintbrush

*1* Layer the cakes (see pages 18–19). Assemble by placing the base slice onto its cake board, adding some ganache to the centre and spreading it towards the edge. Leave the ganache thicker in the middle to form the basis of the dome. Place the next slice of sponge on top and repeat the process with the ganache, building the dome shape each time and tucking down the edges. Repeat with the next two slices. Repeat the layering for the remaining two cakes.

*2* Cover each dome cake with a thin coating of ganache, then coat with marzipan (see page 20), using a cake smoother to create an even surface. Leave to firm overnight.

*With the ganache cream thicker in the centre, add the next sponge layer.*

*Spread the dome-shaped cake with chocolate ganache, using a palette knife.*

*3* Roll out 900g (2lb) milk chocolate paste. Brush the marzipan with clear alcohol, then drape the paste over the largest cake. Work from the top of the dome around and down, ensuring that no air bubbles are trapped. Make sure the surface is smooth and trim off any excess paste. Repeat for the remaining two cakes.

*4* Create an orange-peel effect on the milk chocolate paste covering the domes with a food grater. Using the smallest-holed grater, press firmly onto the chocolate paste, repeating all over each dome and overlapping the impressions many times.

*5* Gently heat the dark chocolate sauce until it is just liquid. Place some in a piping bag (cone), cutting off the end to make a small hole. Pipe the sauce onto the domes, so it is concentrated at the top of the domes and drizzles down the sides. Leave to dry overnight.

*6* Roll out a long strip of chocolate paste. Brush the exposed surface of the cake boards with water and apply the paste to cover. Trim off the excess and, using a small, sharp knife, cut into the paste at 5mm (¼in) intervals to create a pattern. Glue the ribbon to the board edge.

*7* Crown the domes with sugar orange blossom flowers, dark green leaves and sugar oranges, wired together in a spray.

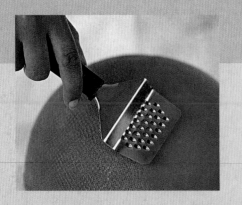

*Create the orange peel effect on the chocolate paste using a food grater.*

*Pipe the dark chocolate sauce onto the top of each cake, allowing it to flow.*

*Decoratively, mark the chocolate paste edging on the cake board with a sharp knife.*

*8* To create the cake stand (see *Stand Ingredients*), roll out the orange sugarpaste (rolled fondant) and cover the 60cm (24in) round cake board. (Brush the board with a little water to help the paste stick to it.) Trim off any excess paste.

*9* Place the cake dummies onto the board, positioning them in such a way that they will show off the cakes to their best advantage. Cut into the sugarpaste around the base of the dummies and remove the sugarpaste circles beneath. Using a hot glue gun, stick the polystyrene to the board in the cut-out circles, making sure that the dummies fit snugly into the holes with no exposed base board.

*10* Roll out the remaining orange sugarpaste to a thickness of about 4mm (¼in). Using a ribbon cutter wheel, cut strips of unequal widths out of the rolled paste. Brush the cake dummies with water and apply the strips, overlapping them in a haphazard way. Trim off any excess sugarpaste.

### STAND INGREDIENTS

2.75kg (6lb) orange sugarpaste (rolled fondant) (see page 150)

60cm (24in) round cake board

15cm (6in) diameter × 10cm- (4in-) deep, 8cm (3in) diameter × 23cm- (9in-) deep and 8cm (3in) diameter × 30cm- (12in-) deep polystyrene cake dummies

Chocolate brown food colouring

*11* Using an airbrush, or a small, soft paintbrush, shade the base board and columns with the chocolate brown food colouring, working from the edges inwards to achieve even coverage. Apply ribbon to the base board edge to match the cakes. Leave the stand to dry for 24 hours before use, then assemble the cakes on the stand.

*The components of the stand – polystyrene cake dummies, sugarpaste, cake board and ribbon.*

*Use a ribbon cutting wheel to cut strips of orange sugarpaste in uneven widths.*

*Using brown food colouring, shade the baseboard and columns with a brush or airbrush.*

This is a chocolate lover's delight, combining moist chocolate cake and a dark ganache filling with a host of incredible textured chocolate decorations. You can choose from a variety of colours and textures to suit your tastes – and those of your guests.

# Textured dream

### CAKE AND DECORATION

900g (2lb) dark ganache (see pages 142–145)

25cm (10in) and 15cm (6in) round chocolate cakes (see pages 138–139)

30cm (12in) and 20cm (8in) round cake boards

750g (1lb 10oz) white marzipan

80g (3oz) cocoa powder

900g (2lb) dark chocolate sauce (see pages 146–147)

450g (1lb) milk chocolate

450g (1lb) dark chocolate

450g (1lb) white chocolate

Gold ribbon for board edge and cake stand

Two-tier off-set cake stand

### EQUIPMENT

Equipment for layering, covering and levelling (see pages 18–21)

Small, soft paintbrush

Greaseproof (wax) paper piping bags (cones)

Equipment for tempering (see pages 16–17)

Thin cotton gloves

Bubble wrap (optional)

Small sponge (optional)

*1* Layer the cakes, filling and coating with ganache and placing them on their cake boards (see pages 18–19. Cover with marzipan (see page 20), level (see page 21) and let firm overnight.

*2* Cut strips of cellophane 1cm (½in) deeper than the height of the cakes and long enough to wrap around them. Lay out the cellophane, brush with water and dust with cocoa powder.

*3* Coat the sides of each cake with dark chocolate sauce. Remove any excess to leave a smooth, thinly coated surface. Pick up the longer cellophane strip at one end and adhere it to

*Layer each chocolate cake with beaten dark ganache, then cover the cake completely.*

*Place the cocoa-coated cellophane strips around the side of the cake.*

the side of the larger cake, with the cocoa powder against the chocolate sauce. Pull the cellophane firmly around the cake, securing it in place with tape. Repeat for the smaller cake.

4 Use a greaseproof (wax) paper piping bag (cone) to flood the top of the cakes with the remaining sauce (the cellophane lip will stop the sauce from overflowing). Leave to stand overnight. Refrigerate for at least one hour before slowly peeling off the cellophane.

5 Temper the milk chocolate (see pages 16–17). Cut six pieces of cellophane of dimensions approximately 30 x 10cm (12 x 4in) and place one on the work surface. Dip two fingers into the chocolate and, without removing any excess, use a stroking action to paint a shape approximately 6cm (2½in) long onto the cellophane, trailing off at the base. Repeat to fill the sheets – about 30 pieces are required for the cakes, but make extra to allow for breakages.

6 As each sheet is filled, take hold of both ends of the strip and gently fold the cellophane 90 degrees lengthways. Lean it up against a baking tray or similar edge to hold the right angle while the chocolate sets. When firm, transfer to the refrigerator for 15 minutes before peeling off the cellophane. Handle with extreme care as the chocolate is very thin and will melt easily with the heat of your hand. (Thin cotton gloves are a useful aid for this, both in handling the chocolate and in preventing marks such as fingerprints.) Place the chocolate shapes in position

*Flood the top of the cake with chocolate sauce using a piping bag. Leave to set overnight.*

*Dip two fingers into the chocolate and paint a shape with a stroking action.*

*Lean the shapes against a baking tray edge. When set, trim the bases to neaten.*

around the sides of the cake so that they stand out like a fringe of petals – using melted chocolate in a piping bag as glue. If necessary, trim the base edges with a sharp knife.

*7* Coat the base boards with some cold chocolate sauce and, using a small palette knife, create another texture. Position the ribbon around the board edges and stick with glue.

*8* Melt the dark and white chocolate (separately) and use them to make some interesting shapes. The decorative pieces on the cake tops are created using triangles cut from different materials (see right), which impart different surface textures. You can create various effects by using different colours of chocolate. Cut out triangles of multiple types and sizes from the materials suggested. Coat one side of the triangles with some melted chocolate using a small, soft paintbrush, then drape them (material-side-down) over several curved surfaces of various diameters and leave until the chocolate sets (rolling pins or cans provide suitable shapes). When set, refrigerate for 15 minutes before gently removing the material from the chocolate. (Wear cotton gloves while handling the triangles, to prevent melting and fingerprints.)

*9* Arrange the chocolate shapes on the top of each cake, securing them in place with a little piped chocolate. Display the cakes on a two-tier off-set stand, which should be trimmed with the same ribbon as the cake board edges.

## Variations

*Here are some suggestions for creating textured decorations with melted chocolate:*

- coat plain cellophane with chocolate of various colours;

- dab-sponge plain cellophane with milk chocolate, then back off with white chocolate. Reverse this chocolate combination or use all three colours of chocolate;

- pipe cellophane with polka dots, then back in with chocolate of another colour;.

- coat bubble wrap with chocolate. When dry, this gives a honeycomb look. Brush with an alternative chocolate first, for a two-tone effect;

- tin foil crinkled up, then smoothed flat and coated with chocolate gives a veined effect;

- textured vinyl wallpaper provides some fabulous surfaces;.

- packaging materials can also be useful. Excellent results can be achieved using the corrugated glassine found in biscuit tins.

*Place the decorative side pieces around the cake, using a little piped chocolate to stick.*

*The cake top pieces are created by using chocolate on various textured surfaces.*

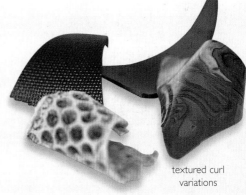

textured curl variations

*This amazing cake is a sweet chocolate celebration, exploding with festivity and fun. A towering centrepiece for any party, you can use any colour chocolate or spirals to suit your preferences. Here, the cake has a fresh and frivolous look, ideal for a light-hearted affair.*

# Carnival cone

## CAKE AND DECORATION

Four 40cm (16in) × 30cm (12in) chocolate cakes (see pages 138–139)

2.4kg (5lb) white ganache (see pages 142–145)

45cm (18in) round cake board

1.4kg (3lb) white marzipan

Icing (confectioner's) sugar for dusting

900g (2lb) white chocolate

Oil-based food colour of your choice

12 gold chocolate dragées

Ribbon for board edge

## EQUIPMENT

Plastic bags

Equipment for layering and covering (see pages 18–20)

Two 30cm (12in) bamboo kebab sticks

Pastry brush

Small, soft paintbrush

Equipment for tempering (see pages 16–17)

5cm- (2in-) wide cellophane strips of various lengths

Notched plastic scraper

Soft cotton gloves

Small piping bag

*1* Place the chocolate cakes into plastic bags and refrigerate overnight to allow them to firm. Cut out 12 cardboard circles, starting with 30cm (12in) diameter and decreasing incrementally by 2.5cm (1in) at a time to end up with a 2.5cm (1in) diameter. Place the circles onto the cakes carefully, in order to minimize wastage, and cut out 12 circles of cake.

*2* Layer the cakes together, sandwiching with ganache (see pages 18–19). Start with the largest circle placed on the cake board, then add cakes of decreasing size, with the smallest at the top. (Too much ganache can cause the cake to slide when straightened, so be sparing.)

*Place the circular templates on the cakes and cut out the circles with a sharp knife.*

*Create a smooth cone shape by trimming off the cake steps with a sharp saw knife.*

*3* Place the cake, on its board, onto a turntable and insert the kebab sticks to help secure the cake while it is shaped. Using a sharp saw knife, start at the top and trim off the cake 'steps' in order to produce a cone shape. Rotate the turntable to sculpt an even shape, then remove the kebab sticks. Brush away the crumbs, using a pastry brush, then apply a thin coat of ganache to the outside of the cake. Work upwards from the base, using short strokes and a little ganache.

*4* Roll out the marzipan into an oblong shape approximately 35cm (14in) x 45cm (18in) x 1cm (½in) thick, using icing (confectioner's) sugar to prevent sticking. Drape the marzipan around the cone cake. It may help to lift the marzipan around a rolling pin first. Butt the joins, applying a little water with a soft paintbrush to ensure good adhesion. Cut away any excess marzipan and smooth with a cake smoother. Allow to dry at room temperature overnight.

*5* To prepare the spirals, temper the white chocolate (see pages 16–17) and colour the chocolate with oil-based food colour. Place a short cellophane strip on a flat work surface and secure at either end with a dot of melted chocolate. (Use different lengths of cellophane to create spirals of various lengths.) Spread a thin layer of chocolate down the centre of the cellophane strip. Using the notched scraper, remove any excess with a smooth action, scraping from one end to the other – leaving an even ribbon. Let the chocolate start to set, but only up to the stage where it is no longer liquid – not long enough for it to solidify and dry.

*Apply a smooth coating of white ganache to the cone, using upward strokes of a palette knife.*

*For the spirals, pipe out coloured white chocolate down the length of a cellophane strip.*

*A notched scraper will give you a neat ribbon width for the spirals.*

*6* Holding both ends of the cellophane strip, twist to form a spiral shape. Using a dot of chocolate, secure each end of the cellophane on a baking sheet to prevent the spirals from unravelling and refrigerate for about 15 minutes.

*7* Remove from the refrigerator and, with extreme care, release the cellophane and unwrap the chocolate spiral. Wear thin cotton gloves to protect against melting the thin chocolate and marking it with fingerprints. Use a small, sharp knife to trim ends and edges that are uneven.

*8* Gently warm the remaining white ganache to around 30°C (85°F). Starting at the base of the cake, apply the ganache using upward strokes. As you work, the ganache will become more viscose and start to set. Long upward strokes with the rounded end of a knife, turning the cake slightly after each stroke, will create decorative ridges. Coat the board with ganache and leave to set. Clean any excess from the board edge with the back of a knife.

*9* Secure the spirals onto the cake and board, using white ganache in a small piping bag (cone) and applying gentle pressure. The ganache should be liquid but cool to the touch, to prevent melting the surfaces that are being joined. Work quickly for best results. Secure the gold dragées with a dot of chocolate to give a scattered effect around the board. Glue the ribbon to the base board edge to complement or contrast with the chocolate spiral colour.

*Curl the cellophane into a spiral shape, secure with chocolate and refrigerate.*

*When dry, you can remove the cellophane strips very carefully to reveal the spirals of chocolate.*

*Attach the coloured chocolate spirals to the cone, using a little white ganache.*

# Truffles

Chocolate truffles are possibly at the pinnacle of chocolate extravagance as they are bite-sized luxuries that melt in the mouth. By adding flavouring and coating, you can tailor-make truffles to suit your own taste or theme.

The heart of a truffle is usually a ganache (see pages 142–145), but you can alter the mixture of ingredients to create different textures – from a light and creamy centre to a dense and intense chocolate experience.

The balance of flavours is extremely important, so when you are adding flavour to your ganache, the strength of the chocolate must be taken into consideration. A light flavour such as champagne or vanilla, works best in either a pale milk or white chocolate ganache, so that the chocolate does not overpower the delicate flavour. Dark rich chocolate, on the other hand, can be enhanced by robust strong flavours, such as coffee or Cointreau.

The appearance of truffles is as important as their taste. Truffles should be dressed on the outside to complement the filling within. You can use chocolate shavings, nuts, powdered chocolate and sugars, or 'spin' with an alternative chocolate colour (see pages 50–53).

*Hearts, the symbol of true love, are ideal accessories on a chocolate wedding cake or for any romantic occasion. The marbled effect on the hearts and the multitude of white chocolate cigarette curls create a glorious cake that is bursting with romance.*

# Hearts and curls

## CAKE AND DECORATION

1.4kg (3lb) ganache (see pages 142–145)

Two 25cm (10in) and four 12cm (5in) round chocolate cakes (see pages 138–139)

40cm (16in) and 12cm (5in) cake boards

1.8kg (4lb) white marzipan

1.8kg (4lb) milk chocolate sauce (see pages 146–147)

3.2kg (7lb) white chocolate

1.25 kg (2lb 12oz) milk chocolate

115g (4oz) milk chocolate paste (see pages 148–149)

Ribbon for board edge

## EQUIPMENT

Equipment for layering, covering and levelling (see pages 18–19)

Six 25cm (10in) bamboo kebab sticks

3 cake dowels

Equipment for tempering (see pages 16–17)

12cm (5in) heart mould

Small, soft paintbrush

Marble slab

Metal (wallpaper) scraper

*1* Layer the cakes, filling and coating them with ganache (see pages 18–19). Place the cakes on their corresponding cake boards – the large cake on the larger cake board and the four small cakes on the smaller cake board, creating a tower. To increase the stability of the tall cake, insert two bamboo kebab sticks.

*2* Cover both cakes with a thin layer of marzipan (see page 20). Using a cake smoother, create smooth straight sides and a flat top with the characteristic rounded top corners. Level (see page 21) and leave the cakes to firm overnight.

*Use a palette knife to make sure that the cake is evenly covered with chocolate sauce.*

*Use a scraper to push the chocolate away from you to form a cigarette curl.*

3 Insert three cake dowels into the centre back of the base cake to support the weight of the tall cake (see page 26). Stand the tall cake on its board and raise it off the work surface. Warm 680g (1lb 8oz) of the milk chocolate sauce, then pour it over the cake so that it is evenly covered – use a palette knife to guide the sauce, if necessary. Leave to stand for approximately 10 minutes until the sauce starts to become firm. Use a palette knife and, with long strokes, form ridges in the coating, working from the bottom to the top of the cake. Repeat for the larger cake, allowing the sauce to coat both the cake and the board. Remove the chocolate sauce from the edges of both cake boards and leave to dry for 24 hours.

4 Temper 225g (8oz) of the white chocolate (see pages 16–17). Use the 12cm (5in) heart mould to produce four half hearts. Polish the mould halves with soft tissue, then dip a small paintbrush into the white chocolate and paint it into the mould in a haphazard fashion. Allow to dry. Temper the milk chocolate and pour into the moulds until level, then refrigerate for 20 minutes. Remove the hearts from the moulds and place them on the work surface.

5 Knead the chocolate paste until it is pliable and roll it into a long, thin 'sausage' shape, about 5mm (¼in) in diameter. With a brush or your finger, spread a little melted chocolate around the edge of the flat surface of the heart, about 1.5cm (just over ½in) in. Working swiftly, stick the chocolate paste sausage onto the melted chocolate around the edge of the heart.

*Secure the chocolate curls to the cake, pushing them into the sauce in a haphazard fashion.*

*Brush the heart moulds with a thin layer of milk chocolate before filling them with the white.*

*6*  Take two kebab sticks and and dip the blunt ends into the melted chocolate about 6cm (2½in) along. Place these sticks, equally spaced, onto the heart – with the sharp ends pointing downwards from the pointed end of the heart. Spread a little more melted milk chocolate onto the chocolate paste sausage, then place the other heart half on top of the first, plain milk sides together, forming a sandwich of the kebab sticks. Press firmly, squeezing the paste to create a join. Trim off any excess paste. Repeat for the second heart. Leave to dry overnight.

*7*  Make the chocolate curls in batches, using approximately 450g (1lb) of untempered melted white chocolate at a time. Spread thinly onto either a marble slab or a metal surface (left at room temperature), using a metal scraper. Massage the chocolate with a forward and backward movement until it becomes firm. Holding the scraper at a 45 degree angle, push the chocolate away from you to form a cigarette curl. You will require about 225 chocolate cigarettes.

*8*  Place the two hearts into position – one on the top of the tall cake, the other on the base cake next to where the tall cake sits. Push the skewers deep inside the cakes, so that even the points of the hearts are pushed into the chocolate sauce. Arrange the white cigarettes around the hearts to form a ruff. Some will push into the sauce, others will need to be secured with melted chocolate. Work your way all around the base board with the curls and allow to firm overnight. Stick the ribbon to the base board edge with glue.

*Push the kebab sticks into the heart half, then secure the other half to create the full heart.*

*Push the kebab sticks into the cake firmly, so that the point of the heart goes into the sauce.*

### Chocolate Tip

For best results, make the white chocolate cigarette curls several hours before they are required. As a general rule of practice, chocolate pieces should always be stored away from the light and placed in an airtight storage box.

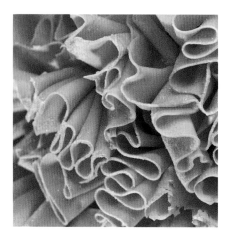

*These stunning white chocolate cakes would look equally good in plain or milk chocolate. Shown here in pristine bridal white, they are a superb combination of the traditional and the unconventional. The wafer-thin ruffles of white chocolate will melt on your tongue.*

# white carnation

### CAKE AND DECORATION

30cm (12in), 23cm (9in) and 15cm (6in) round chocolate cakes (see pages 138–139)

40cm (16in), 32cm (13in) and 25cm (10in) round cake boards

1.8kg (4lb) ganache (see pages 142–145)

2.4kg (5lb) white marzipan

4kg (9lb) white chocolate

80g (3oz) icing (confectioner's) sugar

Gold ribbon for board edges

Three-tier off-set cake stand

### EQUIPMENT

Equipment for layering and covering (see pages 18–20)

Marble slab (small enough to fit in freezer)

8cm- (3in-) wide metal (wallpaper) scraper

*1* Layer the cakes, fill and coat with ganache, then cover with marzipan (see pages 18–20), placing the cakes on their boards. Leave for 24 hours and freeze the marble slab overnight.

*2* Melt the white chocolate, place one of the cakes on a turntable and use a palette knife to coat the cake with a thin layer of chocolate.

*3* When using a frozen marble slab, speed is of the essence, as there is a limited amount of working time before the slab needs to be returned to the freezer. Load a metal (wallpaper)

*Coat each chocolate cake with a thin layer of the melted white chocolate, using a palette knife.*

*Spread the melted white chocolate onto the slab and work with a metal (wallpaper) scraper.*

scraper with melted white chocolate and spread thinly onto the slab. (The frozen slab takes the heat out of the chocolate, causing it to start to set immediately.) While the chocolate is on the slab, cut out a long strip of chocolate, using a knife. Release the strip from the slab by sliding the metal scraper under the piece of chocolate and picking it up with your fingers. The chocolate will still be malleable.

*4* Using the above method, produce enough chocolate strips to position around the sides of the largest cake. Starting close to the top edge of the cake, place the strips in position as you make them, overlapping each other to create a 'peeling' effect.

*5* Produce more chocolate strips, of dimensions approximating 7cm (2¾in) × 30cm (12in) for the carnation top. Remove them from the slab and, using both hands, concertina the chocolate, creating fan-like folds, pinching one edge together to produce a fan shape. Place these on top of the cake around the edge until you have completed a full circle.

*6* Repeat this process to create the carnation effect by building inwards and upwards, stacking the folds. As you build, it is necessary to add 'packing' to the centre of the cake (in the form of folded chocolate) in order to create the raised dome shape. Repeat the process for the remaining two cakes.

*Working quickly, place the white chocolate strips around the side of the cake.*

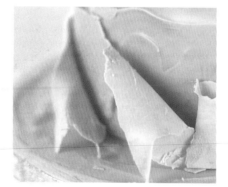

*The chocolate strips on the side of the cake create an attractive, unusual peeling effect.*

*Concertina the chocolate strips creating fan-like folds to be placed on top of the cake.*

*7* Leave the finished cakes to set for about three hours, then dust lightly with icing (confectioner's) sugar, just catching the edges of the folds to create a frosted effect. Attach the ribbon to the board edges using a glue stick.

*8* Display the cakes on an off-set stand (as shown on page 113), where each cake can be seen to its best advantage.

*Dark concertina fans will work equally well on a dark carnation cake.*

## Variations

*Different finishing styles would suit this cake by altering one or several of the components.*

■ You could sprinkle the edges of the carnation with disco violet, paint with gold or silver or lightly dust with cocoa powder.

■ For a beautiful blossoming look, push chocolate roses (see pages 36–37) into the folds of chocolate on the top of the carnation. Use a contrasting-coloured chocolate for the roses, so that they stand out from the chocolate folds.

■ Alternatively, fresh strawberries can be pushed into the folds of chocolate. This works best with white chocolate, as the vibrant red of the fruit contrasts beautifully.

*Position the folds on top of the cake to create a 'carnation' effect.*

*Finally, lightly dust each cake with sifted icing (confectioner's) sugar.*

*This extravagant creation makes a fabulous centrepiece for any celebration. The multitude of brittle chocolate folds and the sumptuous soft sponge create a gorgeous texture combination on the tongue. Your guests will be bowled over by this tree of pure chocolate.*

# Dark ruffles

## CAKE AND DECORATION

Four 40cm (16in) x 30cm (12in) chocolate cakes
(see pages 138–139)

45cm (18in) round cake board

1.8kg (4lb) ganache (see pages 142–145)

1.4kg (3lb) white marzipan

2kg (4lb 6oz) dark chocolate

Ribbon for board edge

## EQUIPMENT

Plastic bags (one per cake)

Equipment for layering
and covering (see pages 18–20)

Two 30cm (12in) bamboo kebab sticks

Pastry brush

Small, soft paintbrush

Marble slab (small enough to fit in freezer)

Metal (wallpaper) scraper

*1* Place the chocolate cakes into plastic bags and refrigerate overnight to allow them to firm. Cut out 12 cardboard circles, starting with 30cm (12in) diameter and decreasing incrementally by 2.5cm (1in) at a time to end up with a 2.5cm (1in) diameter. Place the circles onto the cakes carefully to minimize wastage and cut out 12 circles of cake.

*2* Layer the cakes together, sandwiching with ganache (see pages 18–19). Start with the largest circle placed on the cake board, then add cakes of decreasing size, finishing with the smallest at the top. (Too much ganache can cause the cake to slide when straightened, so be sparing.)

*Cut out the circles of chocolate cake, using a sharp knife and a steady hand.*

*Create the cone shape by slicing off the steps of cake to leave a smooth edge.*

*3* Place the cake, on its appropriate board, onto a turntable and insert the bamboo kebab sticks to help secure the cake while it is being shaped. Using a sharp saw knife, start at the top of the chocolate structure and trim off the cake 'steps' in order to obtain a cone shape. Rotate the turntable to ensure that you sculpt an even shape, then remove the kebab sticks. Brush away the cake crumbs, using a pastry brush, then apply a thin coat of ganache to the outside of the cake. Work upwards from the base of the cone, using short strokes of the palette knife and small amounts of chocolate ganache each time.

*4* Roll out the marzipan into an oblong shape approximately 35cm (14in) x 45cm (18in) x 1cm (½in) thick using icing (confectioner's) sugar to prevent sticking. Drape the marzipan around the cone cake. It may help to lift the marzipan around a rolling pin first. Butt the joins, applying a little water with a soft paintbrush to ensure good adhesion. Cut away any excess marzipan and smooth with a cake smoother. Use long strokes up and down the cone, pushing the soft cake and marzipan into shape. Allow the marzipan covering to dry and firm at room temperature overnight.

*5* Warm the remaining ganache very slightly, so that it is still fairly cool and quite thick – this will be the glue that sticks the chocolate ruffles to the cone. Starting at the top of the cone, coat about one third of the structure with ganache.

*Concertina the chocolate quickly, pinching at one end to create fan-like folds.*

*Fix the fan shapes to the cone cake tightly, leaving no area uncovered.*

*6* When using a frozen marble slab, speed is of the essence, as there is a very limited amount of working time available before the slab needs to be returned to the freezer. Melt the dark chocolate, load a metal (wallpaper) scraper and spread the chocolate thinly onto the marble slab (the frozen slab takes the heat out of the chocolate, causing it to start setting immediately). While the chocolate is on the slab, cut strips of dimensions approximating 8cm (3in) × 30cm (12in), using a sharp knife. Release the chocolate strips from the slab by sliding the metal scraper under the individual pieces and picking them up with your fingers. The chocolate will still be quite malleable.

*7* Using both hands, concertina the chocolate, creating fan-like folds and pinching at one end in order to create a fan shape. Place the fans onto the cone, starting at the top of the cake and working your way around and down. As you reach the end of the 'glued' area, apply some more ganache to create another section to be worked on. (Working in sections will give the ruffles time to set and become secure on the cake.)

*8* When the chocolate ruffles cover the cone completely, coat the cake board around the cake with the remaining ganache. Using a glue stick, trim the board edge with a matching ribbon. Sift icing (confectioner's) sugar over the entire structure in order to achieve a fabulous frosting appearance.

*Sprinkle the finished cake with icing (confectioner's) sugar to emulate snow.*

## Variations

*This cake will look just as stunning in white chocolate as it does in dark. If using it as a centrepiece for a Christmas celebration, you could present this cake adorned with white chocolate ruffles tinted green to resemble a festive Christmas tree.*

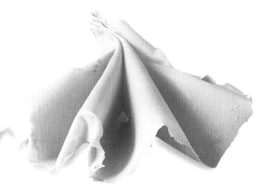

white chocolate variation

*This evocative design is the ideal wedding cake for a couple who has chosen to get married on a tropical island. Many such couples throw a reception for their family and friends when they return and this gorgeous cake is a great way to re-create the paradise island theme of the wedding.*

# Tropical wedding

## CAKE AND DECORATION

30cm (12in) and 15cm (6in) round chocolate cakes (see pages 138–139)

40cm (16in) and 15cm (6in) round cake boards

1.4kg (3lb) chocolate fudge icing (see page 151)

1.4kg (3lb) white marzipan

1.4kg (3lb) white chocolate paste (see pages 148–149)

60g (2oz) milk chocolate

310g (11oz) white chocolate

680g (1lb 8oz) milk chocolate paste (see pages 148–149)

200g (7oz) dark chocolate

225g (8oz) dark chocolate paste (see pages 148–149)

## EQUIPMENT

Equipment for layering, covering and levelling (see pages 18–21)

Equipment for tempering (see pages 16–17)

Seashell mould

Small, soft paintbrush

Greaseproof (wax) paper piping bags (cones)

3 cake dowels

25cm (10in) bamboo kebab sticks

12 artificial leaves (broad silk with wired stems)

Thin wire (optional)

Stiff-bristled paintbrush

*1* Layer the cakes, fill and coat with fudge icing, then cover with marzipan (see pages 18–20). The top-tier cake is placed on a cake board of the same size, the edges of which should be covered as well. Level (see page 21), leave to dry overnight, then coat both cakes with white chocolate paste, including the board of the base cake. Leave to dry overnight.

*2* Temper the milk chocolate (see pages 16–17). Apply the tempered chocolate to the shell mould with a small brush, creating a haphazard layer of chocolate and leaving gaps for the white chocolate to show through. Temper the white chocolate, place into a piping bag (cone)

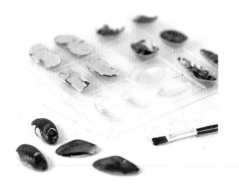

*Brush the shell moulds lightly with milk chocolate before filling them with white chocolate.*

*Push the chocolate paste pieces onto the kebab sticks to form the trunks of the palm trees.*

and fill the shell shapes. Leave to set for at least 20 minutes, placing in the refrigerator for the final 10 minutes. To de-mould, invert the mould sheet over a clean work surface and tap it gently – the shell pieces will fall out. Reserve until required. (You will need about 25 shells.)

*3* Insert three cake dowels into position in the base cake (see page 26). Place the top cake (on its board) into position, off-centre and to the back of the base cake. Insert two bamboo kebab sticks into the smaller cake at slight angles to each other.

*4* Knead 225g (8oz) of the milk chocolate paste until it is pliable. Roll into a sausage 1.5cm (⅝in) thick and cut the sausage into 2cm (¾in) slices. Roll each into a ball, then pinch each piece at one end. Thread the balls over the kebab sticks, narrow-end-down, repeating until you have built two palm tree trunks (you may wish to use a little water to ensure a good bond). Snip off any uncovered kebab stick, level with the last piece of chocolate paste.

*5* To create the leaves, use six large silk flower leaves for each tree. Cut out the characteristic V-shapes along the edges and strip off the plastic coating from the stem of each leaf to reveal the thin wire. Temper the dark chocolate (see pages 16–17) and, using a small paintbrush, paint both sides of each leaf and allow to dry. Gather three leaves together and twist their wires to form one stem. Repeat this with the other leaves, then put two 'threes' together, again twisting

*Paint the silk flower leaves with tempered dark chocolate and allow to dry.*

*Attach the leaves to the chocolate paste trunks using the twisted wire stems.*

*Knead the milk chocolate paste until it is pliable and workable, ready for rolling.*

the wires to form one stem. Insert the wire into the top of the tree trunk and repeat for the other tree. (Twist a wire around the kebab stick and the leaf wires to anchor them in position.)

*6* Knead 50g (2oz) of the dark chocolate paste until pliable. Roll into a sausage and cut into 9 pieces. Roll these into coconut-shaped balls and drop two or three as if fallen from the trees. Secure the others with melted chocolate at the tops of the trunks. Leave to firm overnight.

*7* Place a fan of kebab sticks onto the base cake. Roll out the remaining milk chocolate paste into an oblong about 5mm (¼in) thick, brush a little water between the sticks to anchor the paste, then drape the paste over the sticks. Using a small, sharp knife, trim off the excess, level with the base cake top. Push the paste into shape over the sticks to form waves.

*8* Knead the remaining dark chocolate paste until pliable. Roll out into an oblong 30cm (12in) x 8cm (3in). Cut out the shapes from the wave template with a sharp knife. Butt around the top cake, resting on the milk chocolate paste. Leave overnight, then remove the kebab sticks.

*9* Using a little tempered milk and dark chocolate and a stiff-bristled paintbrush, dab patches of chocolate in a random pattern over the sides of both cakes. Place the moulded chocolate shells around the base board and hold each in position with a spot of melted chocolate.

*Once the paste has dried overnight, remove the kebab sticks from beneath the 'waves'.*

*Dabbing with tempered chocolate will create a natural sandy look for your cake.*

*Three stacked chocolate cakes create a tiered effect, their lipped ledges brimming over with fresh fruits. Here, they are filled with delicious juicy red grapes and a scattering of redcurrants for additional colour, but sumptuous variations can be created using any soft fruit in season.*

# Parcel cake

## CAKE AND DECORATION

30cm (12in), 23cm (9in) and 15cm (6in) square chocolate cakes (see pages 138–139)

40cm (16in), 30cm (12in), 23cm (9in) and 15cm (6in) square cake boards

2.75kg (6lb) ganache (see pages 142–145)

2.4kg (5lb) white marzipan

3.6kg (8lb) white chocolate

5cm- (2in-) wide cream-coloured waterproof florist's ribbon

2.4kg (5lb) red grapes

4 punnets redcurrants

## EQUIPMENT

Equipment for layering, covering and levelling (see pages 18–21)

Marble slab (small enough to fit in freezer)

8 cake dowels

Equipment for tempering (see pages 16–17)

6 sheets cellophane

Metal (wallpaper) scraper

Triangle template for corners (see pages 152–155)

Greaseproof (wax) paper piping bag (cone)

*1* Layer the cakes, fill and coat with ganache (see pages 18–19). Put each cake on its board and place on spare boards while you are working. Apply a coating of marzipan to each cake, including the cake board edge (see page 20). Use a cake smoother and ensure straight-angled corners. Level (see page 21) and leave to dry for at least 24 hours. Freeze the marble slab.

*2* Insert four cake dowels into each one of the two larger cakes (see page 26). Place the marzipanned 30cm (12in) cake onto the 40cm (16in) base board. Stack the remaining two cakes (on their boards) squarely on top.

Layer and cover the cakes (including their boards) with a layer of ganache.

Roll out the tempered white chocolate between sheets of cellophane.

*3* Temper the white chocolate (see pages 16–17). Take a sheet of cellophane and place it onto the work surface. Pour about 450g (1lb) of chocolate onto the sheet, cover with a second sheet, then take a rolling pin and roll the chocolate through the cellophane, spreading it into a very thin layer. Leave to cool and dry for at least 30 minutes.

*4* Measure the sides of each cake and add an extra 1.5cm (⅝in) to the height. Cut three oblong card templates (one for each cake) to match the dimensions of the sides of each cake (including the extra height). Remove the top layer of cellophane from the sheet of chocolate. Place an oblong template onto it and use a craft knife to cut through both the chocolate and its backing sheet. Cut four pieces for each template – one for each side of each cake. Attach the chocolate oblongs to the sides of the cakes using a little tempered chocolate (ensure that the cellophane sides are facing outwards). Once the chocolate has set, peel away the cellophane in a swift movement to result with an unblemished glossy side with no fingerprints.

*5* Take the marble slab from the freezer and spread some white chocolate quickly and evenly onto it using a metal (wallpaper) scraper. The chocolate will set almost immediately because the heat and temper will be taken out of it by the cold slab. Place a corner template onto the set chocolate and cut around the shape. Release the shape from the slab by running the scraper under it. (Handle the chocolate carefully and quickly, as it is very unstable in this state.)

*Using templates, cut out oblongs of tempered white chocolate for the sides of the cakes.*

*Use a triangle template to produce the 'folded' corners of each parcel.*

*Bend the chocolate triangles into shape around the corners of the cake.*

Place into position on the corner of the cake, bending into shape. Repeat for the remaining 11 corners. As the chocolate warms in the heat of the room it will almost melt again, but it will still hold its shape. After approximately one hour, it will have regained its stability and become quite firm.

*6* Double over the ribbon, so that it is 2.5cm (1in) wide and stick it together with a glue stick. When dry, stick the stiff ribbon around the base board edge.

*7* Place some tempered white chocolate in a piping bag (cone). Starting at the top, flood the 15cm (6in) cake top, followed by the ledges around the three tiers, including the base board. Ensure that all the marzipan is sealed in under a thin layer of chocolate. Leave to dry.

*8* Place the fresh fruit into position on the ledges of the tiers as close as possible to the time of presentation, so that the juice does not have a chance to stain the white chocolate.

### Cake Tip

This parcel cake can be prepared a few days in advance. As with most chocolate wedding cakes, it should be stored at room temperature (15°C [60°F]).

*9* To create the topknot of white chocolate trellis, drizzle some white chocolate over a strip of cellophane (see page 93). Drape the cellophane over a rolling pin until the chocolate is set, then carefully peel off the cellophane. Place several pieces of latticed chocolate on top of the fruit to create the desired look.

*Glue the folded ribbon all around the base board edge, creating a recess.*

*Flood the recess with tempered white chocolate, leaving enough room for the fruit.*

*This spectacular towering centrepiece for your celebration is certainly a showstopper. Having been stunned by the splendid overall effect, your guests can pick their own individual mouth-watering chocolate and orange mousses from the tree — simplicity itself.*

# Orange tree

## CAKE AND DECORATION

3.5kg (7lb 12oz) milk chocolate

550g (1lb 4oz) chocolate mousse powder

570ml (9fl oz) fresh whipping cream

25cm (10in) x 40cm (16in) chocolate cake
(see pages 138–139)

300 tinned mandarin orange segments

800g (1lb 12oz) orange-coloured
white chocolate paste (see pages 148–149)

## EQUIPMENT

Equipment for tempering (see pages 16–17)

5cm- (2in-) tall dariole moulds

5cm (2in) plain round cutter

Savoy bag

1cm (½in) plain savoy tube (tip)

1 Temper the milk chocolate (see pages 16–17) and mould into 150 individual hollow cups (see page 15). You can produce these in advance, over a few days.

2 Assemble the stand (see *Stand Ingredients*). Start with the 38cm (15in) cake board at the bottom. Fix the 30cm (12in) polystyrene dummy on to this, using the hot glue gun to secure in position. (The ledge created at the bottom will help to support the oranges around the base.) Next, glue the 60cm (24in) board into place, ensuring that it is centrally positioned. Glue three of the small polystyrene dummies in a triangular cluster at the centre of the board. On top of

*Mould the tempered chocolate into cups, by filling the cups and pouring back the excess.*

*Assemble the stand using the cakes boards and the polystyrene cake dummies.*

## STAND INGREDIENTS

38cm (15in), 60cm (24in), 50cm (20in), 40cm (16in), 30cm (12in), 20cm (8in) cake boards

30cm (12in) diameter x 25cm- (10in-) deep polystyrene cake dummy

Hot glue gun

Eight 8cm (3in) diameter x 9cm- (3½in-) deep polystyrene cake dummies

1kg (2lb 4oz) dark chocolate

2.5cm (1in) paintbrush

50 fresh oranges (medium or small)

Fresh or silk fern leaves

36 bamboo kebab sticks

Edible gold powder or spray

these pieces, glue the 50cm (20in) cake board. Glue another three polystyrene pieces in the middle of this board. On top of these pieces, glue the 40cm (16in) board, then glue one polystyrene piece in its centre. Top this with the 30cm (12in) board with the one remaining dummy glued at its centre. Finally glue in place the 20cm (8in) board to form the top shelf.

**3** Temper the dark chocolate and, using a paintbrush, coat the boards and polystyrene of the stand. Cover all the surfaces with a coat of chocolate, including the board edges. Leave to dry.

**4** Fill the chocolate cups with mousse filling on the day of the wedding and keep refrigerated. Place 155ml (4½fl oz) of cold water into a mixing bowl. Add the chocolate mousse powder, whisking with a hand whisk until smooth. Add half the whipped cream, whisk until half blended in, then add the remaining cream and clear through. Do not over-mix as splitting will occur.

**5** Using a plain round cutter, cut circles from the chocolate cake, then slice each piece into six thin layers. Put some chocolate mousse into a savoy bag fitted with a 1cm (½in) plain tube (tip) and pipe a small bulb into the base of each chocolate cup. Place two mandarin segments on top, then cover with another bulb of chocolate mousse to within 5mm (¼in) from the edge. Close the cup by pressing a slice of chocolate sponge into position. Turn the cup upside-down onto its new base, then place on a tray to refrigerate. Repeat for the remaining cups.

*Coat the entire stand (boards and dummies) with a layer of tempered dark chocolate.*

*Fill the chocolate cups with their layers of flavours – mousse, mandarin and more mousse.*

*Seal each chocolate cup with a disc of chocolate cake, pushed in firmly.*

*6* To make the decoration on top of each cup, take 115g (4oz) of the orange-coloured chocolate paste and roll it into a 'sausage'. From this strip, cut 100 pieces, roll each into a ball, then place three together in order to form a triangle with a fourth placed on top to obtain a pyramid shape. If you put them together as you roll them, they will require no additional 'glue' but, if necessary, a tiny amount of water may be used. Place one decoration on top of each chocolate cup, securing in place with a small dot of melted chocolate. Repeat five times to produce 150 decorations.

*7* On the day of the celebration, dress the stand with fresh oranges and fresh or silk fern leaves. Place the first orange on the ledge of the base board, leaning against the polystyrene dummy. Insert a kebab stick into one side of the orange and through into the polystyrene to hold it in place. Use the wire cutters (snips) to cut off any protruding stick. Butt the next orange into position as close as possible to the first and repeat the skewering and cutting process. Work your way around the base, then move out to form a second and third layer.

*8* When all the oranges are in position, paint a few of them with edible gold. You may also wish to paint a few of the chocolate decorations on some of the cups. Using a glue gun, fasten the fern leaves into position amongst the oranges – this will soften the overall appearance and add natural colour to the stand. Place the chocolate pots into position on the stand.

## Variations

*As an alternative to chocolate mousse, you could fill the cups with ganache (see pages 142–145). It is slightly heavier and richer in taste but works well with the mandarin oranges. If you choose to add a touch of alcohol to this dessert, marinate the mandarin oranges for a couple of days in the spirit of your choice.*

*Roll pieces of orange-coloured chocolate paste between your fingers to create tiny oranges.*

*Use the kebab sticks to secure the fresh oranges to the cake stand, snipping off any protrusions.*

*Place the individual chocolate and orange desserts onto the ledges of the stand.*

*These simple chocolate place settings will add a personal touch to your celebration. Those shown here take their themes from cakes featured in this book, creating continuity across your table setting. Your guests may not want to eat their personalized masterpieces, but take them home instead!*

# Place settings

## INGREDIENTS

255g (9oz) chocolate (milk, white or dark) for every 10 guests

One chocolate paste rose per guest (see pages 36–37)

30g (1oz) contrasting-coloured chocolate (milk, white or dark) for every 10 guests

## EQUIPMENT

Equipment for tempering (see pages 16–17)

Cellophane sheets

Greaseproof (wax) paper piping bags (cones)

## Roses

*1* Temper the first chocolate and spread it 3mm (⅛in) thick onto a cellophane sheet. Leave to dry and then, using a small, sharp knife, cut into oblong pieces about 9cm (3½in) × 4cm (1½in).

*2* Place a chocolate paste rose (see pages 36–37) at one end of the oblong, securing with some melted chocolate.

*3* Melt the contrasting-coloured chocolate and pipe the names of the guests onto the settings.

Rose place setting

Create the chocolate paste roses as described on pages 36–37.

Make sure that the chocolate roses are in proportion with your oblong settings.

## INGREDIENTS

500g (1lb 2oz) chocolate (milk, white or dark) for every 10 guests

100g (3½oz) chocolate paste for every 10 guests (see pages 148–149)

30g (1oz) contrasting-coloured chocolate (milk, white or dark) for every 10 guests

Edible gold or silver (optional)

## EQUIPMENT

Equipment for tempering (see pages 16–17)

Cellophane sheets

Greaseproof (wax) paper piping bags (cones)

## INGREDIENTS

450g (1lb) chocolate (milk, white or dark) for every 10 guests

100g (3½oz) contrasting-coloured chocolate milk, white or dark) for every 10 guests

One white chocolate cigarette curl per guest (see page 24)

One small, round truffle per guest (see pages 50–53)

## EQUIPMENT

Equipment for tempering (see pages 16–17)

Cellophane sheets

Triangle template (see pages 152–155)

Round metal cutter

Greaseproof (wax) paper piping bags (cones)

op art triangle

tent

## Tents

*1* Temper the first chocolate and spread it 3mm (⅛in) thick onto a cellophane sheet. Leave to dry and then, using a small, sharp knife, cut into oblong pieces about 9cm (3½in) x 4cm (1½in). Cut two pieces for each tent and join them together with melted chocolate at the top to form the tent shape.

*2* Roll a little chocolate paste into a long sausage. Cut in half, and roll the two pieces together to form a twisted rope. Trim a length to fit along the top of each tent. Fix into place along the top of the tent using a little melted chocolate.

*3* Melt the contrasting-coloured chocolate and pipe each tent with the name of a guest. As an alternative to piping, the names can be written with edible gold or silver using a paintbrush.

## Op art triangles

*1* Temper the first chocolate and spread it 3mm (⅛in) thick onto a cellophane sheet. Leave to dry and then, using a small, sharp knife, cut into oblong pieces about 9cm (3½in) x 4cm (1½in).

*2* Melt the contrasting-coloured chocolate and spread onto a cellophane sheet. Cut one triangle shape for each setting and, using a warmed metal cutter, cut a small hole into each.

*Erect the tents using melted chocolate and secure paste ropes to the tops.*

*This variety of shapes and textures creates a striking and delicious op art setting.*

*3* Take one white chocolate cigarette curl for each setting and prop it against the triangle with the end protruding through the hole. Position the triangle at a diagonal to the corner of the oblong. Secure in place with a little melted chocolate.

*4* Place a truffle at the base of the triangle, securing it in place with some melted chocolate. Personalize this contemporary place setting by piping the name of each guest using melted chocolate of a contrasting colour.

## Lollipops

*1* Temper the first chocolate and pipe a flat bulb onto a sheet of cellophane by squeezing the piping bag gently, keeping it at a low angle and quite close to the cellophane.

*2* Insert a lollipop stick – laying it on the chocolate surface, twisting to coat it with chocolate, then pressing it gently down to just below the surface of the chocolate. Make sure that it does not pass right through the chocolate and protrude on the other side.

*3* Leave the lollipops for about 20 minutes to dry. Remove from the cellophane by holding the stick and gently peeling the paper away. Pipe names or designs on the flat side of the lollipops in melted chocolate of a contrasting colour.

### INGREDIENTS

400g (14oz) chocolate (milk, white or dark) for every 10 guests

30g (1oz) contrasting-coloured chocolate (milk, white or dark) for every 10 guests

### EQUIPMENT

Cellophane sheets

One lollipop stick per guest

Greaseproof (wax) paper piping bags (cones)

Pipe out the flat bulbs of tempered chocolate, keeping them as uniform as possible.

Insert the sticks carefully, pressing them into the centres of the chocolate bulbs.

lollipops

# BASE CAKES, SAUCES and ICINGS

Cakes, fillings, coatings, sauces and icings are the elements that hold together the celebratory chocolate creations in this book. You can choose the recipes for these components to complement the cake that you are creating. For example, you can choose from rich or light cakes and ganache, dark, milk or white chocolate sauces and pastes.

# Base cakes

The chocolate base cakes for the creations in this book should be as sumptuous as you can make them. There are some great chocolate cake mixes available from supermarkets, but if you are after that unique home-made flavour, try one of the following recipes. Use the recipes as guides – for each, the full recipe produces two 25cm (10in) round cakes. Use one third of the recipe to produce two 15cm (6in) round cakes; half for two 20cm (8in) round cakes and the full recipe plus one third for two 30cm (12in) cakes. Simply select a different tin for square cakes, octagonal cakes and oblong cakes.

## Light chocolate cake

This is a fairly basic, light recipe, using cocoa powder for the flavour. Ideal for the seasonal wedding cakes (see pages 78–81 and 86–89).

### INGREDIENTS

225g (8oz or 1cup) vegetable margarine, plus extra for greasing

370g (13oz or 3¼ cups) self-raising flour, plus extra for the tins

450g (1lb or 2 cups) caster (superfine) sugar

30g (1oz) salt

140 g (5oz) cocoa powder

4 medium eggs

285ml (10fl oz) evaporated milk

285ml (10fl oz) warm water

1 Preheat oven to 180°C (350°F).

2 Grease cake tins with vegetable margarine and sprinkle with flour.

3 Sift together the dry ingredients and rub the vegetable margarine into them until the mixture resembles fine breadcrumbs.

4 Beat the eggs thoroughly and stir them together with the evaporated milk and warm water.

Stir the evaporated milk and warm water into the egg mixture.

5 Combine the egg mixture and the dry mixture and beat well.

6 Pour the mixture into the cake tins and bake for about 35 minutes or until firm.

7 Leave in the tins for a few minutes before removing to a cooling rack.

## Rich chocolate cake

This is a gloriously rich cake that is somewhat heavier than the previous recipe. This would be a great base cake for the Dark ruffles cake (see pages 116–119).

### INGREDIENTS

Vegetable margarine for greasing

400g (14oz or 3½ cups) self-raising flour, plus extra for the tins

370g (13oz or 1⅔ cups) butter

370g (13oz or 2¼ cups) dark soft brown sugar

8 large eggs

225ml (8fl oz) warm water

225g (8oz) dark chocolate

15g (½oz) salt

1 Preheat oven to 180°C (350°F).

2 Grease cake tins with vegetable margarine and sprinkle with flour.

*1* Preheat oven to 180°C (350°F).

*2* Grease cake tins with vegetable margarine and sprinkle with flour.

*3* Sift together the flour and cocoa powder.

*4* Fill a medium-sized saucepan one third full of water and bring to a gentle simmer. Combine the eggs and sugar in a metal mixing bowl and place this over the pan. Stir until the mixture is warm to the touch.

*5* Lift away from the saucepan and use an electric mixer on medium speed until the mixture triples in volume (about 8 minutes). When the whisk is lifted, a thick trail of mixture should be left behind.

*6* Gently fold in the dry ingredients, then melt the butter and fold it in.

*7* Pour the mixture into the cake tins and bake for about 25 minutes or until firm.

*8* Leave in the tins for a few minutes before removing to a cooling rack.

*3* Cream together the butter and sugar until light and fluffy. Separate the eggs and beat the yolks until light.

*4* Melt the chocolate and add with the water to the yolks – mix until combined.

*5* Add the egg mixture to the sugar batter and stir thoroughly, then sift the dry ingredients and fold them through the egg and sugar mixture.

*6* Whisk the egg whites until they are at soft peak stage. Fold carefully into the mixture without over-working.

*7* Pour the mixture into the prepared cake tin(s) and bake for approximately 30 minutes or until firm.

*8* Leave in the tins for a few minutes before removing to a cooling rack.

## Moist chocolate cake

This cake has a great consistency, ideal for the Textured dream (see pages 98–101).

### INGREDIENTS

Vegetable margarine for greasing

300g (10½oz) plain (superfine) flour, plus extra for the tins

185g (6½oz) cocoa powder

15 large eggs

500g (1lb 2oz) caster (superfine) sugar

70g (2½oz) unsalted butter

*A thick trail of sugar-and-egg mixture should be left behind on the whisk.*

# Cake flavours

*For an extra dimension to your base cake, you can add a hint of flavour. Look at the other ingredients in the cake creations to make sure that a flavoured base cake will be complementary. The following recipes will produce two shallow 25cm (10in) round cakes. Halve the recipe to make two 20cm (8in) round cakes, or use one third to make two 15cm (6in) cakes.*

## Coffee cake

This is a great idea as a base cake for the Cappuccino cloches (see pages 42–45).

**INGREDIENTS**

340g (12oz or 1½ cups) vegetable margarine, plus extra for greasing

340g (12oz or 3 cups) self-raising flour, plus extra for the tin(s)

340g (12oz or 1½ cups) caster (superfine) sugar

6 large eggs (at room temperature)

30g (1oz) or 3 heaped teaspoons instant coffee

*1* Preheat oven to 180°C (350°F).

*2* Grease cake tins with vegetable margarine and sprinkle with flour.

*3* Cream the margarine and sugar to achieve a light and fluffy consistency.

*4* Dissolve the coffee, adding just sufficient boiling water to make it liquid.

*5* Beat the eggs thoroughly and add to the sugar mixture, beating in a little at a time. Add the dissolved coffee as you add the last of the egg.

*6* Sift the flour thoroughly and gently fold it into the mixture.

*7* Pour the mixture into the prepared cake tins and bake for approximately 30 minutes or until firm.

*8* Leave in the tins for a few minutes before removing to a cooling rack.

## Orange cake

You could use this fruity-flavoured cake as a complementary base cake for the Orange domes (see pages 94–97) or Orange tree (see pages 128–131) recipes.

Follow the recipe for the coffee cake, but substitute ten drops of orange oil and the grated rind and zest of one whole orange for the coffee. This will give a delicious, subtle orange flavour with little flecks of colour. If you prefer an orange-coloured cake, add a few drops of food colouring at the creamed margarine and sugar stage.

*Coffee is an interesting flavour variation to a chocolate base cake.*

# Ganache

This rich chocolate filling is at its best if prepared the day before use and left to stand overnight. In this book, this basic recipe is used in three different ways.

## Filling and coating cakes

When the ganache has matured for 24 hours, warm it very slightly to soften it. Using an electric mixer, beat on a fast speed until the ganache is aerated, soft and has turned a much paler colour. Then, spread on slices of chocolate cake to layer them together (see pages 18–20).

## Pouring to cover cakes

Simply put the ganache mixture in a saucepan over a low heat and warm slightly – to no hotter than 35°C (95°F). Then, pour over the cake to cover (see page 20).

## Filling truffles

Using mixture that is 24 hours old, pipe small bulbs of ganache onto a sheet of greaseproof (wax) paper to form the creamy centres of these delicious chocolate treats (see pages 50–53).

Unless specified otherwise, the ganache used for the cakes in this book is milk chocolate ganache, but you can use dark or white chocolate as a variation. You may need to make minor adjustments to the quantity of chocolate, depending on the type used. As a rule, more white chocolate is required and less dark chocolate.

Here are three simple ganache recipes to choose from:

## Standard ganache

This is a great recipe for making a simple but delicious ganache – ideal for filling, coating, pouring and putting into truffles.

*Ganache is used as the creamy chocolate filling between layers of cake.*

*Spread over the top and sides of a cake it keeps the sponge moist and adheres to the marzipan.*

### INGREDIENTS

800g (1lb 12oz) chocolate

45g (1½oz) liquid glucose

220ml (7fl oz) fresh whipping cream

1  Melt the chocolate to 40°C (105°F).

2  Combine the liquid glucose and fresh cream in a saucepan and bring to the boil.

*3* Add the boiled glucose and cream mixture to the melted chocolate and stir thoroughly to combine.

*4* Allow the ganache to cool, then transfer to an airtight container and refrigerate.

## Light ganache

For a lighter cream, you can use this standard recipe and add an extra dimension. This is a good option for filling and coating very rich and creamy cakes – to lighten them. Try it with Pipes and scrolls (see pages 66–69) or the Textured dream cake (see pages 98–101).

### INGREDIENTS

800g (1lb 12oz) chocolate

45g (1½oz) liquid glucose

220ml (7fl oz) fresh whipping cream

1kg (2lb 4oz) butter cream

*1* Melt the chocolate to 40°C (105°F).

*2* Combine the liquid glucose and fresh cream in a saucepan and bring to the boil.

*3* Add the mixture to the melted chocolate and stir thoroughly.

*4* Allow to cool and then stir in the butter cream until combined.

*5* Transfer the light ganache to an airtight container and refrigerate.

## Swiss ganache

This recipe uses butter to produce a much richer and more luxurious ganache that is ideal for filling truffles. You can add some alcohol, if you like, to give this delicious ganache an extra kick.

### INGREDIENTS

800g (1lb 12oz) chocolate

45g (1½oz) liquid glucose

220ml (7fl oz) fresh whipping cream

60g (2oz or ¼ cup) unsalted butter

125ml (4fl oz) alcohol (optional)

*For a simple cake (left), just layer and coat with ganache, then sprinkle with cocoa powder.*

*Add the boiled liquid glucose and cream mixture to the melted chocolate and combine.*

*1* Melt the chocolate to 40°C (105°F).

*2* Combine the liquid glucose, cream and butter in a saucepan and bring to the boil, making sure that the butter is melted in.

*3* Add the glucose, cream and butter mixture to the melted chocolate and stir through thoroughly.

*4* Allow the ganache to cool and add alcohol (if using).

*5* Transfer the Swiss ganache to an airtight container to refrigerate.

*A coating of ganache should be fairly thin (right), but should seal in the entire sponge.*

### Ganache Tip

Ganache will keep for six months in an airtight container in the refrigerator.

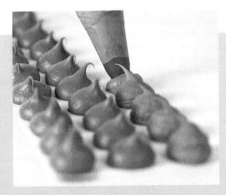

*Swiss ganache is the perfect choice for rich, buttery truffle centres.*

# Chocolate sauce

*Sauces can be used for pouring over cakes or for serving with slices of cake as an extra taste dimension to the dish. Choose from the following recipes:*

## Coating sauce

This sauce is a kind of ganache and is an excellent medium for pouring over cakes. Although it sets, it retains elasticity, so it will not crack. It has great texture and flavour.

### INGREDIENTS

4g (⅒oz) or 1 leaf gelatine

280ml (9fl oz) milk

100g (3½oz) liquid glucose

300g (10½oz) (any combination of dark, milk and white) chocolate

300g (10½oz) cooking chocolate

*1* Soak the leaf gelatine in a small amount of warm water, then leave until cold.

*2* Bring milk and liquid glucose to the boil, then add the cooled leaf gelatine mixture.

*3* Melt the chocolate and cooking chocolate, and add to the gelatine mixture. Place in an airtight container overnight.

*4* When ready to use, warm the sauce to 35°C (95°F) and pour over the cake. (This sauce will keep for six months.)

## Rich serving sauce

This is a beautifully rich sauce, particularly when made with dark chocolate. It makes the perfect accompaniment to a truly decadent cake, such as the Croquembouche tower of profiteroles (see pages 38–41).

### INGREDIENTS

570ml (19fl oz) fresh whipping cream

450g (1lb) dark or milk chocolate

115g (4oz or ½ cup) unsalted butter

*1* Put the cream in a heavy-based saucepan and bring to the boil over a gentle heat.

*The basic components of a chocolate coating sauce – milk, liquid glucose and chocolate.*

*A rich dark sauce is gorgeous served warm and poured over profiteroles.*

*Add the butter to the chocolate and cream mixture and whisk until smooth.*

*2*  Add the chocolate and stir until melted.

*3*  Add the butter to the chocolate and cream mixture and stir until melted, then whisk until smooth. Serve immediately.

## Custard-based sauce

This sauce is a kind of rich chocolate custard, but by thinning it with milk, you can create the sauce consistency you desire.

### INGREDIENTS

960ml (32fl oz) full-cream milk

3 eggs

80g (3oz) caster (superfine) sugar, plus extra for sprinkling

30g (1oz or ¼ cup) cornflour (cornstarch)

115g (4oz) dark chocolate

*1*  Put the milk in a heavy-based saucepan and bring to the boil over a gentle heat.

*2*  Combine the eggs, sugar and sifted cornflour and whisk until pale.

*3*  Pour the boiling milk slowly over the egg mixture and whisk until combined.

*4*  Return to the saucepan and bring back to the boil, stirring to achieve sauce consistency.

*5*  Sprinkle with caster sugar, cover with greaseproof paper and cool for 15 minutes.

*6*  Remove the paper, melt the chocolate and stir it in. Reheat before serving.

# Chocolate paste

*Chocolate paste can be used as an alternative to marzipan for covering cakes or as a final coating. You can also use it to make shapes, such as roses. (It will keep for six months in an airtight container – without refrigeration.) The cakes in this book call for pastes of different colours:*

## Dark paste

A very rich paste, used in cakes such as Rose drape (see pages 32–35)

### INGREDIENTS

600g (1lb 6oz) dark chocolate

200g (7oz) liquid glucose

50ml (1¾fl oz) water

*1*  Warm the chocolate to 40°C (105°F).
*2*  Warm the glucose slightly, add to the chocolate and mix well, then add the water.
*3*  Place in a plastic bag and leave to stand overnight to become solid.
*4*  To use, cut into small pieces and knead.
*5*  For a very smooth paste, pass through the rollers of a pasta machine several times.

## Milk paste

A rather milkier paste that is used in cakes such as Orange domes (see pages 94–97).

### INGREDIENTS

800g (1lb 12oz) milk chocolate

200g (7oz) liquid glucose

50ml (1¾fl oz) water

Follow the steps for the dark chocolate paste, but use milk chocolate instead of dark chocolate.

*The components of a milk chocolate paste – water, liquid glucose and milk chocolate (here shown in callet – or drop – form).*

## White paste

This is a more sugary paste, but comes out a creamy white – used for cakes such as Rose drape (see pages 32–35) and Spring wedding (see pages 72–73), in which the paste is tinted green..

### INGREDIENTS

750g (1lb 8oz) white chocolate

200g (7oz or ⅞ cup) granulated sugar

100ml (3½fl oz) water

370g (13oz or 3¼ cups) icing (confectioner's) sugar

*1*  Warm the chocolate to 40°C (105°F).
*2*  Make a simple syrup with the sugar and water, by mixing them together and bringing them to the boil.
*3*  Add the chocolate to the syrup and mix thoroughly, then add the icing (confectioner's) sugar to the mixture.
*4*  Place in a plastic bag and leave to stand overnight to become solid.
*5*  To use, cut into small pieces and knead.
*6*  For a very smooth paste, pass through the rollers of a pasta machine several times.

# Chocolate sugarpaste

Sugarpaste (rolled fondant) can be used for covering cakes and for producing detailed chocolate shapes and textures. Any recipe that uses chocolate paste for covering or decoration can be substituted with sugarpaste. You can vary the colour by altering the proportions of icing (confectioner's) sugar and cocoa powder – a darker paste, for example, requires more cocoa powder and less icing sugar. This recipe makes about 700g (1lb 9oz) of sugarpaste, but for larger quantities, you can buy it ready-made. Sugarpaste will keep for three months in an airtight container – it need not be refrigerated.

## INGREDIENTS

30g (1oz) egg white made from albumen powder

225g (8oz or 2 cups) cocoa powder

60g (2oz) liquid glucose

450g (1lb or 4 cups) icing (confectioner's) sugar, plus a little extra, if required

30g (1oz or 2 tbsp) white vegetable fat, plus a little extra, if required

1  Add the egg white to the liquid glucose and mix together thoroughly.

2  Sift together the cocoa powder and icing (confectioner's) sugar twice, to ensure that the cocoa is well mixed. Add to the egg mixture and mix until combined.

3  Turn the mixture onto a work surface and add the white fat, kneading well until the paste is smooth and pliable.

4  You can adjust the consistency, as required, by adding a little more sieved icing sugar or white vegetable fat.

5  Wrap the sugarpaste in a plastic bag to keep completely airtight before storing it.

6  When ready to use, simply cut off a portion of the sugarpaste and knead it gently until it is pliable.

Coloured chocolate sugarpaste is great for creating striking details on cakes and stands.

# Chocolate fudge icing

*This is used as an alternative to ganache for filling and coating cakes and is used in cakes such as Pipes and scrolls (see pages 66–69). It will keep for about three months in an airtight container – it does not need to be refrigerated.*

## INGREDIENTS

450g (1lb) block fondant

30ml (1fl oz) water

100g (3½oz) icing (confectioner's)sugar, plus a little extra, if required

30g (1oz) cocoa powder

30g (1oz) milk powder

100g (3½oz) white vegetable fat

75g (2¾oz) dark chocolate

*1* Soften the fondant with the water, so that it is workable.

*2* Put the fondant, the icing (confectioner's) sugar, the cocoa powder, the milk powder and the vegetable fat into an electric mixer. Beat on a medium setting for two minutes.

*3* Melt the chocolate and add it to the other ingredients. Scrape down the sides of the bowl, so that all the ingredients are in the centre, before beating thoroughly for a further 4 minutes.

*4* If necessary, you can adjust the consistency of the fudge icing, by adding a little more icing sugar.

*5* Wrap the icing in a plastic bag to keep completely airtight before storing.

*Chocolate fudge icing produces rich-looking, elaborate pipework.*

# *Templates*

*Kemet pyramid accessories*

*(pages 62–65)*

cartouche

triangle

*Croquembouche stars*

*(pages 38–41)*

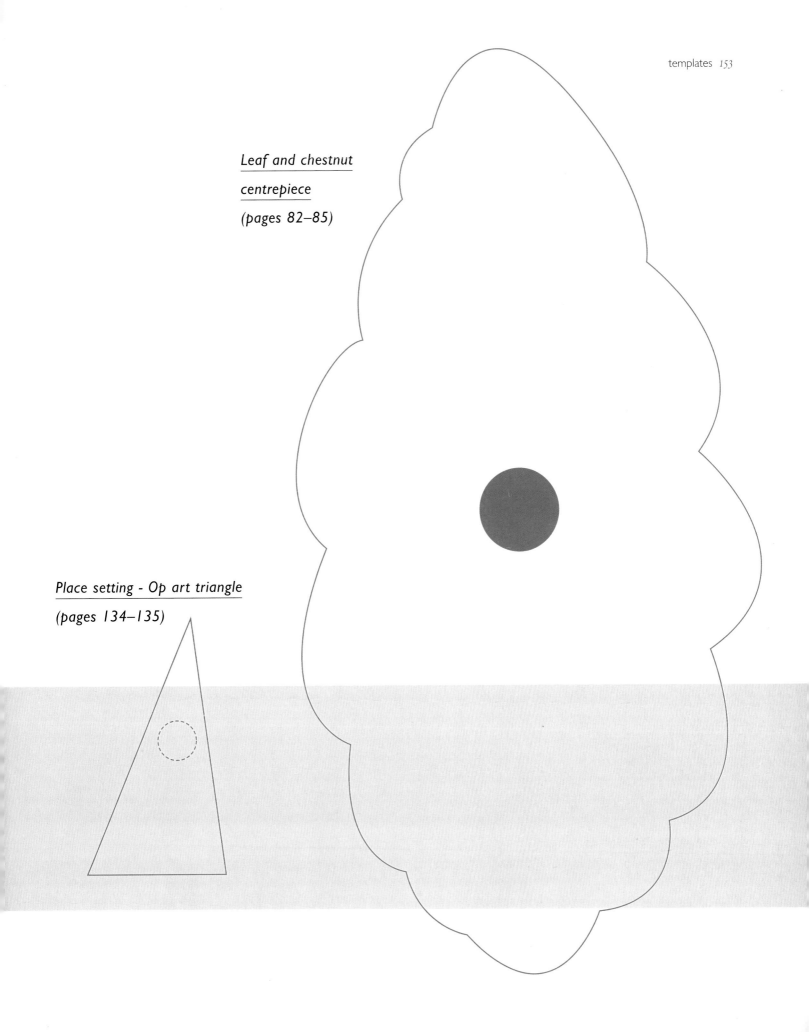

*Leaf and chestnut*

*centrepiece*

*(pages 82–85)*

*Place setting - Op art triangle*

*(pages 134–135)*

*Parcel cake triangles*

*(pages 124–127)*

## Winter wedding snowflakes

### (pages 86–89)

*Piping white chocolate over these templates will produce beautifully detailed chocolate snowflakes.*

# Index

# Suppliers

Contact the following companies to source chocolate equipment via mail order or to find the whereabouts of your local supplier.

*For good Belgian chocolate:*

**Barry Callebeaut (UK)**

Wildmere Road Industrial Estate

Banbury

Oxen OX16 7UU

Tel: 01295 224 700

Fax: 01295 273 294

*For good Belgian chocolate and edible gold and silver aerosols:*

**Slattery Pâtissier and Chocolatier Ltd**

190 Bury New Road

Whitefield

Manchester M45 6QF

Tel: 0161 767 9303

Fax: 0161 796 7334

Email: john.slattery@virgin.net

Website: www.slattery.co.uk

*You can also purchase good Belgian chocolate at most sugarcraft shops and some supermarkets.*

*For disco violet and other colourings:*

**Edible Art**

County Durham DL1 66LZ

Tel/Fax: 01388 816 309

*For block fondant and chocolate mousse powder:*

**Sparkling Sugarcraft Supplies**

361 Bury Old Road

Prestwich

Manchester M25 1PY

Tel/Fax: 0161 773 3033

*For tempering thermometers and other small equipment:*

**Home Chocolate Factory**

Rosedale House

Rosedale Road

Richmond

Surrey TW9 25Z

Tel: 020 8939 9000

Fax: 020 8940 9504

Website: www.homechocolatefactory.com

*For professional chocolate moulds:*

**JKV**

Post Bus 7

5126ZG

Gilze

Holland

Tel: 01615 2290

Fax: 01615 1655

**Gerhard Ruth**

GmbH

Mettemichstr 7

D44867

Bochum Wattenscheid

Germany

Tel: 023 27320414

Fax: 023 2733939

# Acknowledgements

*This book is dedicated to my dad, **Bernard Slattery**.*

*Without his faith and encouragement, his trust and guidance, my love*

*of the confectionery craft would not have blossomed.*

*I miss him.*

*Thanks to those listed below, without whose help this book would have taken a lot longer*
*to write and definitely would not have been as good:*
*My wife, Marilyn, who puts up with me and my work (the same thing really).*
*My daughters, Kate and Laura, who both make a 'mean' chocolate cake.*
*My mum, Margaret, who dedicated many years of her life to building our business.*
*John Costello, my chocolatier, who did a great deal of the preparation work for the photographs in this*
*book. I am sure you will appreciate the quality of his work. (Oh, and thanks to Jenny for letting him.)*

*A very big thanks to all the rest of my staff at* Slattery Pâtissier & Chocolatier, *who keep the*
*business running while I occasionally take my 'eye off the ball':*
*Dave, Pat, Karen, Nicky, Mal, Wendy, Anne, Mark W, Mark C, Louise, Kerry, Colin, Mogda, Sue, Kim,*
*Maxine, Deb, Barbara, Alma, Mel, Robert and Ensi.*

*Elizabeth Gough who made the beautiful sugar flowers for the* Spring wedding cake.
*Stephen and Ann Barnes (*Slattery of Manchester*) for cake bases and the use of the van.*
*Daffs Florist (*Whitefield*) who created the fresh flower arrangements for the* Summer wedding cake.

First published in 2001 by Merehurst Limited

Merehurst is a Murdoch Books (UK) imprint

Copyright © 2001 Merehurst Limited

Photographs © Merehurst Limited

ISBN 1-85391 879 2

A catalogue record for this book is available from the British Library.

**Commissioning Editor:** Barbara Croxford

**Design & Art Direction:** Helen Taylor

**Project Editor:** Dawn Henderson

**Photographer:** Laurence Hudghton

**Stylist:** Cath Garrick

**CEO:** Robert Oerton

**Publisher:** Catie Ziller

**Publishing Manager:** Fia Fornari

**Production Manager:** Lucy Byrne

**Group General Manager:** Mark Smith

**Group CEO/Publisher:** Anne Wilson

Colour separation by Colourscan, Singapore

Printed in Singapore by Tien Wah Press

**Murdoch Books (UK) Ltd**
Ferry House, 51–57 Lacy Road,
Putney, London, SW15 1PR
Tel: +44 (0)20 8355 1480
Fax: +44 (0)20 8355 1499

*Murdoch Books (UK) Ltd is a subsidiary
of Murdoch Magazines Pty Ltd.*

**Murdoch Books®**
GPO Box 1203, Sydney,
NSW 1045, Australia
Tel: +61 (0)2 4352 7025
Fax: +61 (0)2 4352 7026

*Murdoch Books® is a trademark
of Murdoch Magazines Pty Ltd.*